THE TEXAS

7

St. Martin's Paperbacks
True Crime Library Titles
by Gary C. King

THE TEXAS 7
AN EARLY GRAVE

THE TEXAS

7

A TRUE STORY
OF MURDER AND
A DARING ESCAPE

GARY C. KING

St. Martin's Paperbacks

THE TEXAS 7

Copyright © 2001 by Gary C. King Enterprises, Inc.

Cover photographs courtesy AP/Wide World Photos/Texas Dept. of Criminal Justice, File.

ISBN: 0-312-98157-0

Printed in the United States of America

St. Martin's Paperbacks edition / April 2001

10 9 8 7 6 5 4 3 2 1

For Virgil and Dixie King

ACKNOWLEDGMENTS

I would like to gratefully acknowledge Beale Dean, Esq., of Fort Worth for taking the time out of his busy schedule to help keep me updated on the news in Texas as it occurred.

I am also grateful to Judi Jones Perry for her efforts in alerting me to the late-breaking news about this case, and for her magnanimous efforts in helping me get the word out about my books.

I would also like to thank my agent, Peter Miller, of PMA Literary and Film Management, and his development associate, Kate Garrick, for bringing the particulars of this deal together, and for all of their hard work, and everyone at PMA for helping me further my true-crime writing career.

ACKNOWLEDGMENTS

I am also indebted to Charles E. Spicer, Jr., Executive Editor at St. Martin's True Crime Library, for having the vision to quickly identify the Texas 7 case as an important book and for being able to push it through the wheels of business without encountering the usual kinks in the machinery. I am also very grateful to his assistant editor, Joe Cleemann, for his top-notch skills, talent, and high energy level that enabled pulling this all together in short order. I'd also like to express my sincere appreciation to Anderson Bailey for his help in putting together a terrific photo insert in the short timeframe within which we had to work.

Finally, as always, I want to thank Teresita, Kirsten, and Sarah for standing behind me with their love and patience and the sacrifices they have made to help me finish this project in a timely fashion.

"Let no guilty man escape . . . "
—ULYSSES S. GRANT

AUTHOR'S NOTE

The following story unfolded quickly over several weeks, and it is my hope that its presentation here unfolds just as quickly for the reader as it did for me. It is a true story, and this is a true account of it. None of the names have been changed.

Some of the dialogue is based on witness statements that appeared in both the news media and official reports, including, but not limited to, the Texas Department of Criminal Justice, Institutional Division. Other sources include the Federal Bureau of Investigation and the Irving, Texas, Police Department. Other dialogue is quoted from a variety of sources— *The Dallas Morning News; Fort Worth Star-Telegram; The New York Times; The Houston*

AUTHOR'S NOTE

Chronicle; The Denver Post; The Associated Press; CNN; CBS News; MSNBC; and ABC News, all of which did an outstanding job reporting this exciting, fast-breaking story which is still unfolding even as I write these words. I have made every attempt to re-create the events in chronological order, and have included as many elements of the story as time and my publication schedule allowed.

—G.C.K.

February 2001

CHAPTER
1

Kenedy is located in the southern part of Texas, some 62 miles southeast of San Antonio. With a population of 3,763, it is the largest city in Karnes County, serving as an economic hub for the outlying agricultural and ranching area. First called Kenedy Junction when it was founded as a town site in 1886, Kenedy grew up rapidly due to its position as a major stop on the San Antonio and Arkansas Pass Railroad. With growth came bad guys, mostly gun-fighters, and by the turn of the century Kenedy was being referred to as "Six-Shooter Junction." With little else besides agriculture and ranching to support its economy, the area remained primarily rural and was eventually outgrown by communities in other parts of the state.

After the United States entered World War II, the community became the home of the Kenedy Internment Camp. Originally a Civilian Conservation Corps Camp, the internment camp materialized after the U.S. Government persuaded a number of Latin American countries to deport people of German, Japanese, and Italian ancestries to the U.S. so that they could be exchanged for Allied prisoners, particularly for those in Japan. The first 700 or so internees arrived in April 1942, and the camp housed about 2,000 internees by the following year. The Japanese internees ran a 32-acre vegetable farm located nearby, and the German internees ran a slaughterhouse. Today a residential area occupies the site.

Nearly a century after being nicknamed "Six-Shooter Junction," Kenedy still has a large number of bad guys in its midst. Few people paid them any mind, however, because everyone believed that they were safely confined, with little or no chance of escape, behind the walls of the John Connally Unit—a maximum-security prison located just outside of town and operated under the jurisdiction of the Texas Department of Criminal Justice. Until recently most people outside the region hadn't even heard of Kenedy, Texas. That all changed on Wednesday, December 13, 2000, when seven of society's lowest dregs would stage a brazen, commandolike prison break, a breakout that was orchestrated with such military precision and efficiency that some would speculate it must have taken a year or longer to plan.

December 13 turned out to be a particularly cold day in Kenedy. The temperature remained below 30 degrees during the early morning hours, between midnight and four A.M., and it only warmed up to the low forties by that afternoon. It rained more than an inch in South Texas that morning, and the temperature brought the threat of freezing rain. Because of the inclement weather conditions, prisoners of the Connally Unit's inside yard squad were not required to turn out for their work duties. Other prisoners, however, whose work duties were normally performed indoors, were not affected by the weather restriction.

George Rivas, 30, inmate number 702267, was serving 99 years for aggravated kidnapping and burglary committed in El Paso, and he was tired of life behind prison walls. Although he had attained trustee status and a job in the prison's maintenance department, considered one of the best duty assignments in the prison, he had become disheartened by the grim prospect of never walking the streets a free man again, of spending his nights confined to an austere 8' × 8' cell equipped with only a bunk, a wash basin, and a toilet. He was sick of the lousy food that was typically served in the mess hall, and he was tired of hearing the metal doors slide shut after he returned to his cell at lockdown. Rivas had been making plans for some time, along with six other inmates, to do something about it, and he had decided that this was the day to carry out his plans.

It was 11:20 A.M. when guards and supervisors returned 20 inmates who were assigned to the maintenance department, to their housing areas. Then the guards and supervisors went to lunch, which was what Rivas and his cohorts had counted on. Earlier, these five had convinced Patrick Moczygemba, a maintenance supervisor, to allow them to remain behind to wax and seal the maintenance department's floors. That, they figured correctly, would be effective in keeping most of the other prisoners, as well as the guards, out of the area. They had also convinced Moczygemba to allow them to take their lunch in a "picnic spread" in the maintenance area and to use food that they had purchased at the commissary, instead of eating with the rest of the prison population in the dining area. It was a privilege afforded the best-behaved inmates, and Moczygemba had agreed to allow them this "luxury." Since it was not uncommon for this group of prisoners to be assigned special projects in the maintenance department, Moczygemba agreed to stay and watch Rivas, as well as Joseph Garcia, 29, Randy Halprin, 23, Larry Harper, 37, and Donald Newbury, 38, while the other supervisors went to lunch. Mark Burgess, another maintenance supervisor, allowed one of the inmates under his authority, Patrick Murphy, 39, to also remain in the department for lunch to assist the others in completing the project.

Another inmate, Michael Rodriguez, 38, who was

in on the plan, had been assigned to the inside yard squad that day, but due to the inclement weather he was forced to abide by the weather-related work restriction that the rest of his squad was under. However, Rodriguez had previously made an appointment to visit the law library, which he kept that particular morning. After about an hour, he checked out at 9:40 A.M., and was subsequently, albeit inadvertently, allowed through the gate at the A turnout area. There he gained access to the maintenance area (where he was not supposed to be) after telling guards that he had been assigned to pick up trash. Rodriguez spent much of the remainder of the morning sitting on a bench just outside the maintenance department, where several prison employees later recalled seeing him. No one, except for the escapees, knew that he had positioned himself as the lookout for the other six inmates while they put their plan into motion.

By 11:30 A.M. there was no turning back. Moczygemba, dressed in a gray-and-black flannel shirt, Wrangler blue jeans, a Ranger belt, and brown Red Wing boots, was sitting at his desk in the maintenance office when Rivas came in and got his attention.

"You're needed in the warehouse," Rivas told him.

Without questioning Rivas, Moczygemba pushed his paperwork aside and got up from his desk. When he reached the warehouse, located behind the maintenance department, the other inmates were busy clearing the floor so that they could begin waxing and sealing. Nothing seemed to be amiss, and when Moc-

zygemba asked why he was needed, Harper joined
Rivas and pointed to a large motor on the floor, beneath a table.

"What should we do with that motor?" Harper
asked without a trace of uneasiness in his voice as he
gestured toward the motor. "We need to get it off the
floor."

As Moczygemba leaned down to look at the motor,
one of the inmates, brandishing an ax handle, rushed
over and struck him in the head.

The blow rendered him momentarily unconscious.
Then, as he regained some of his senses, the dazed
and blurry-eyed Moczygemba began to struggle with
the inmates. Garcia ended the scuffle by holding a
handmade knife to the supervisor's neck.

"A few more years to our sentences don't mean
anything to us," Garcia said. "We'll kill you if we
need to."

Moczygemba stopped struggling, and the inmates
proceeded to remove his pants and shirt. Afterward
they tied his hands and legs, shoved a gag inside his
mouth, and placed a pillowcase over his head. They
then carried him to the electrical room at the back of
the warehouse where they forced him to lie facedown
on the floor.

The inmates also stole his sunglasses, watch, keys,
and his wallet, which contained several credit cards
and $30 cash. They also took two blue Texas De-
partment of Criminal Justice coats from his office, as
well as a camouflage cap and a blue ski cap. His keys

gave them access to the sensitive tools room where they stole several pairs of wire-cutting pliers, two hacksaws, a bolt cutter, and a utility knife. Rodriguez, who had been standing guard outside the maintenance department, was then allowed inside, where he would assist the others in the next stage of Rivas's escape plan.

Minutes later, at 11:45 A.M., Alan Camber, another maintenance supervisor, and Alejandro Marroquin, a corrections officer, returned from lunch and sat down at their desks inside the maintenance office. Rivas, Halprin, Harper, Murphy, and Newbury entered and began talking to them. As part of the group spoke to Marroquin, Murphy and Garcia questioned Camber regarding a part they said they needed for a vacuum cleaner. After gaining the two men's attention, Rivas walked behind Marroquin and grabbed him in a bear hug while, simultaneously, Garcia attacked Camber from behind.

As Marroquin struggled to break free Halprin, Harper, and Newbury helped Rivas force him to the floor. After removing his uniform and shoes, they quickly bound the officer's hands and legs with plastic ties and duct tape, and attempted to place a gag inside his mouth. When he refused to open his mouth Newbury punched him in the nose. That opened his mouth, and they placed the gag inside. After robbing him of his watch, keys, identification card, and $65 cash, they carried Marroquin to the electrical room and placed him on the floor next to Moczygemba.

Rivas, meanwhile, helped Garcia force Camber to the floor. Garcia placed a sharp, pointed object in Camber's left ear and threatened to shove it all the way in if Camber did not quit struggling. Fearing for his life, Camber did as he was told and allowed the prisoners to remove his black Wrangler jeans and his boots. After stealing his keys, pocketknife, wallet containing his prison identification, and $60 cash, they bound him just like the others and dragged him into the electrical room where they slammed his head against an electrical conduit on the wall, knocking him out cold. They placed a pillowcase over his head and wrapped duct tape around it in the area of his eyes.

By noon, Manuel Segura and Mark Burgess, having finished with their lunch, were on their way back to the maintenance department. Shortly after arriving back at their offices, Rivas entered and approached Burgess.

"Mr. Moczygemba is in the warehouse and needs to see you," Rivas said.

Having no reason to disbelieve him, Burgess followed Rivas to the warehouse. When he entered the warehouse, Burgess saw no sign of Moczygemba. As he was about to say something, Halprin, kneeling down by the motor beneath the table, called for Burgess to take a look at it.

"We need to know what to do with this motor," Halprin said.

As Burgess walked toward Halprin, one of the

other inmates struck him in the back of the head with the ax handle. He fell to the floor and momentarily lost consciousness. As he began to come around, Burgess felt something sharp at the back of his neck, at his back, and below his right armpit.

"This is no joke," Rivas told him. "We go home, and you go home, or not. It's up to you."

Garcia placed what appeared to be a Plexiglas shank—or homemade knife—in Burgess's left ear and threatened to apply force if he didn't remain quiet and cooperate. Then, just like the others, Halprin proceeded to remove Burgess's clothing, bind his feet and hands, place a gag inside his mouth and duct tape over his eyes, and drag him to the electrical room with the others. Halprin also took Burgess's wallet, which contained his driver's license, Social Security card, and a credit card. Rivas used the same ruse to get Segura into the warehouse, and he was likewise taken captive. Segura was visibly shaken and scared, fearing for his life.

"If you calm down and stay quiet," Rivas told Segura, "nothing will happen to you."

By 12:20 P.M. the seven prisoners had been carrying out their escape plans for an hour when Jerry McDowell, a recreational program specialist often referred to as the "Coach," walked into the maintenance department and found Rivas, Halprin, and Murphy sitting in the office, alone and unsupervised.

"Why are you guys alone?" McDowell asked.

"Mr. Moczygemba went to 18 dorm," Rivas told him. "He'll be back in a few minutes."

McDowell apparently believed him, and asked to check out a toolbox. Murphy volunteered to go to the warehouse to get the toolbox and the checkout log. When he returned he handed both items to Halprin, who in turn passed them to McDowell. The coach signed the log, wrote in the time, turned, and walked out with the toolbox. Thinking that perhaps he should be added to their collection of captives, Rivas followed him out of the office and asked him to come back. But McDowell refused the request and continued out of the area.

Five minutes later, at 12:25 P.M., three additional maintenance supervisors returned from lunch. Mark Garza, Martin Gilley, and Ronny Haun walked into the maintenance department, each paying the convicts little or no mind. Gilley went into the electrical shop, Garza sat down at his desk in the office, and Haun walked into the warehouse. As with the others, the convicts took them captive one at a time.

"Mr. Haun, could you please take a look at this?" Newbury asked as he pointed toward a shelf in the warehouse.

As Haun walked toward the shelf in question, Newbury grabbed him and placed him in a headlock. Rivas moved in quickly and helped Newbury force him to the floor and attempted to place a gag inside his mouth. As Haun struggled, Rivas punched him twice in the nose. When he cried out in pain, Rivas shoved the gag inside his mouth. But the supervisor continued to struggle with his attackers until another inmate held a Plexiglas knife to the back of Haun's left ear. Haun then settled down and allowed the prisoners to bind his arms and legs. Then he was carried to the electrical room.

While Haun was being subdued, convict Harper walked into Garza's office and asked him to come into the warehouse to take a look at the motor beneath the table and he was taken captive in turn. Simultaneously, Garcia walked into the electrical shop where Gilley was working.

"Would you like something to eat, Mr. Gilley?" Garcia asked.

"No, thanks," Gilley responded.

Garcia walked out of the shop as if everything was okay. Moments later Murphy entered the electrical shop.

"Mr. Moczygemba wants to see you in the warehouse," Murphy said.

Gilley followed Murphy, and upon entering he warehouse he was attacked by Garcia, Halprin, Newbury, and Rodriguez.

"Don't resist and you won't be harmed," Halprin told Gilley. Gilley submitted and removed his clothes, was bound and taken to the electrical room with the others.

At 12:40 P.M., an hour and twenty minutes into the operation, another maintenance supervisor, Terry Schmidt, returned from lunch escorting two inmates,

David Cook and Roger Fishwick, from the cellblock to the maintenance department for a work detail. Rivas met them, and told Schmidt that Mr. Moczygemba needed to see him in the warehouse right away. Upon entering the warehouse, several of the escapees attacked Schmidt from behind.

While Schmidt was being subdued, Murphy went inside the maintenance office and began talking to inmates Cook and Fishwick.

"We're having a spread in the back," Murphy said. "Why don't you guys come on back and fix yourselves a plate?"

Fishwick declined the offer, but Cook immediately went to the back of the warehouse where Rivas met him and punched him in the face. Although dazed, Cook swung back at Rivas. Sensing that Rivas might need some help, one of the other inmates rushed over and struck Cook in the back of the head with the ax handle that they had been using. Murphy, meanwhile, went back to the maintenance office and forced Fishwick inside the warehouse where he, too, was struck in the back of the head with the ax handle. Cook and Fishwick were then bound like the others and taken to the electrical room.

Five minutes later, at 12:45 P.M., Randy Albert, a correctional officer, walked into the maintenance office to check out a hitch for his unit's utility vehicle, commonly referred to as a gator. Assigned to the trash crew that day, Albert needed the hitch and the gator to haul lumber. Albert was somewhat disturbed when he entered the maintenance office and saw only inmates present without any supervision. He knew that sometimes the supervisor would go to the warehouse and leave an inmate in the office area alone, a violation of the prison system's rules and regulations but not uncommon. He knew that the rule was often bent by many prison employees, and he was not overly disturbed.

"Where is Mr. Moczygemba?" Albert asked.

"He's in the warehouse," Rivas told him.

When Albert entered the warehouse, he saw no sign of Moczygemba, only inmates. As he looked around he saw a handheld radio and a set of keys on the floor, and immediately sensed that something was very wrong. Before he could act, however, three of the inmates attacked him from behind and forced him to the floor. One of them placed a knife against his face and warned him not to move. Albert grabbed the knife and bent the blade, but he was quickly struck alongside the head with an ax handle. While he was dazed, the inmates handcuffed him with his own handcuffs, bound his legs with rope and tape, and dragged him off to the electrical room.

"We cut off ears for souvenirs," Rodriguez told Albert, loudly enough that the others could hear, too. "And there's lots of ears in here!"

At 1:00 P.M., Lester Moczygemba, another maintenance supervisor with the same last name as his colleague, and another inmate, Ambrosio Martinez, returned to the maintenance department from the boiler room to dispose of a piece of metal. Upon entering the department Moczygemba noticed that the prison's maintenance truck had been pulled into the shop area, where the overhead door was closed and locked. He immediately thought it strange that the truck was parked there because vehicles were not normally allowed in that area without a specific reason, like moving supplies. As Moczygemba was looking around the area, Newbury came up behind him brandishing a flat piece of metal, about 12 inches in length and sharpened on both ends.

"You'd better stop while you're ahead," he said to Newbury as he pushed the inmate's hand away. Then Moczygemba turned toward Martinez and Newbury came up behind him and placed a handmade knife to his throat.

"I'm very serious," Newbury told him. "I don't want to hurt you, but I will if you don't lie down and cooperate."

Fearing for his life, Moczygemba complied and lay down on the floor. Newbury and Halprin then bound his hands and feet, placed a pillowcase over his head, and took him to the electrical room to join the others. As Moczygemba was being hauled off, Murphy attacked Martinez and stabbed him on his left ring finger with the homemade knife. Afterward, Rivas and Garcia bound Martinez's arms behind his back with duct tape and placed him with the others.

Satisfied that they had accounted for everyone who

might cause them problems, the seven escapees secured the electrical room door from the outside and
set into motion the next phase of their daring escape
plan.

CHAPTER

2

Although Rivas and his gang had only been at it for an hour and 55 minutes, the passage of time seemed like an eternity as they made their desperate bid for freedom. But he was confident that they were going to make it. His plan, so far, had gone off without a hitch. As Rivas was getting ready to put the next phase into action, however, a substantial noise emanated from behind the electrical room door, where he and the others had placed their captives.

Unknown to Rivas and his cohorts, maintenance supervisor Terry Schmidt had been able to free himself from his restraints and had begun helping the others free themselves. Mark Garza had been carrying a pocketknife that the convicts had not found when they took him captive, and Schmidt had been able to use the knife to cut the duct tape and plastic ties from his colleagues' arms and legs. The only person he was unable to free was Randy Albert, who had been hand-cuffed.

The captives began feverishly tearing the electrical conduit from the walls to prepare for the possibility that their assailants might return. They used the conduit to barricade the door from the inside, and decided that it could also be used as a weapon to defend themselves if the inmates did, in fact, decide to come back.

It became apparent to the escapees that their captives had managed to get out of their restraints when one of the inmates attempted to enter the electrical room but found that the door, which opened into the room and not outward, had been barricaded. They realized that for their escape to be successful, they had to make certain that their captives could not get out of the electrical room. Thinking quickly, Rivas and one of the other convicts secured a cable to the door and used a winch to keep it closed.

Afterward, Rivas, impersonating a supervisor, telephoned the A turnout officer, the number 3 building desk officer, and the 18-19 turnout officer, and informed each that only a skeleton crew of prisoners would return to their job assignments after lunch was finished. He reasoned that by making such a phone call it would lessen scrutiny on the maintenance department and decrease their chances of being found out before making their break for freedom.

At 1:05 P.M. a correctional officer assigned to the prison's central control area telephoned the maintenance department and asked to speak with a supervisor. It was time for one of the dozen daily head counts. Rivas answered the call, and instructed one of the other inmates to come to the phone to impersonate Patrick Moczygemba. The central control officer advised the man he thought was Patrick Moczygemba that it was time to call the lieutenant for the count. When the inmate placed the call, he was careful to include the three inmates who had been subdued with the prison employees, as well as Rodriguez, who did not work in the maintenance department, along with Rivas and the other five. That would ensure that the head count would balance.

At 1:15 P.M., correctional officer Lou Gips, assigned to the back gate picket and radio tower, received a telephone call from someone who identified himself as a supervisor in the maintenance department. The back gate picket is a narrow, fenced area reinforced with razor wire that leads to the back gate and the outside perimeter road. Gips was informed by the caller that maintenance employees would be entering the area to install monitors in the picket zone. The telephone call, as well as the description of the work order, seemed legitimate to Gips because he recalled that similar work had been recently performed at one of the other picket zones in a different area of the prison. As a result, he had no reason to question the work order.

Meanwhile, three inmates who remained behind in the maintenance area took care of business at their end, under Rivas's instructions. Rodriguez remained outside as a lookout, while one of the other prisoners made the necessary telephone calls to the other prison areas. Rivas, earlier, had worked feverishly building a plywood and cardboard shelter in the back of the truck, which had been brought into the compound earlier in the day in anticipation of a trip into town that afternoon for supplies. The shelter would be used for his accomplices, particularly those dressed in prison whites, to hide in during the trip out through the gate and into town.

At 1:20 P.M., another correctional officer, Vernon Janssen, received a telephone call similar to the one that Gips had received, presumably from a supervisor in the maintenance department. Janssen, who was assigned to the back gate sally port, was told that a maintenance crew would be installing monitors at the back gate area. The sally port is a narrow, fenced-in gateway or passageway that separates the picket area and is used to keep inmates separated from the vehicles that use the picket area to gain access to other prison areas. The call seemed legitimate and, like Gips, Janssen had no reason to question the proposed work.

As all of the telephone calls were being made to set up the next phase of the escape plans, one of the captives, Alan Camber, made an attempt to let the central control officer know that something was very wrong by setting off a fire alarm from the electrical room. The correctional officer on duty made several attempts to contact the department by telephone, but there was no answer. Assuming that it was a false alarm, the officer silenced it from the control panel.

Minutes later, at 1:40 P.M., Rivas and Halprin, dressed in civilian clothing taken from the maintenance supervisors, showed up at the back gate picket area in the department's gator, a utility vehicle similar to a golf cart, along with two inmates dressed in prison uniforms. The two men in prison clothing climbed off the vehicle and, following procedure so they would not arouse suspicion, used the sally port to walk to the pedestrian gate. Expecting the maintenance workers because of the earlier telephone call, Lou Gips opened the walk-through gate and allowed the inmates to enter the fenced area behind the gatehouse. He then opened the vehicle gate and permitted the gator carrying Rivas and Halprin to proceed into the vehicle area. Gips failed to check the men's identification, however, a violation of prison policy.

Rivas and Halprin climbed out of the gator and they entered the gatehouse with monitors and electrical wire. They opened the back door of the gatehouse and allowed their two fellow inmates to enter. Before Janssen could ask for identification, Halprin began examining an electrical outlet in the office area near Janssen's desk. As he was doing so, the telephone on the desk rang and Halprin answered it. Unknown to Janssen, the phone call had been placed by one of the inmates who had remained behind in the maintenance department. Posing as a maintenance supervisor, he wanted to know whether the crew had arrived at the back gate. Halprin handed the phone to Janssen, throwing him off guard and further delaying any attempts that he might make in requesting identification.

As Janssen leaned over to take the call, Rivas grabbed him from behind, placed him in a headlock, and forced him to the floor. His attackers removed his pants and shoes, bound his arms and legs, taped his mouth with duct tape, carried him into the gatehouse restroom, and secured the door from the outside.

Satisfied that Janssen could not escape, Halprin walked up to the exterior gate and identified himself as a maintenance worker. Officer Gips looked around from his vantage point above the compound to make certain that there were no inmates in the area and, recalling that he had seen one of the maintenance supervisors earlier that day dressed in the same clothing and cap, and thinking that this was the same person, opened the outside gate and unwittingly allowed Halprin to leave the area. He then opened the picket door, which allowed Halprin to enter the tower. As Halprin climbed the tower stairs, the telephone rang. When Gips answered, the caller identified himself as a maintenance supervisor.

"Has the maintenance staff arrived at your location?" the caller asked. "I need to speak to one of them."

When Halprin took the phone and began talking,

he removed his jacket and placed it on a chair in the tower and at the same time grabbed a .357 caliber revolver that was lying on the desk. Halprin pointed the gun at Gips.

"This is an escape," he said. "You need to cooperate if you don't want to get hurt."

Murphy, one of the inmates dressed in prison whites, yelled up at the tower to open the gate. But Halprin didn't know how to operate the controls.

"You either show me how to open the picket door and vehicle gate," Halprin told Gips while pointing the gun at him, "or I'm going to kill you."

Fearing for his life, Gips complied.

"Now where are the rest of the guns?" Halprin asked.

Gips told him that they were stored at the bottom of the tower. Halprin ordered Gips to go downstairs and show him, after which Halprin used Gips's belt and shoestrings to tie him up. Murphy then collected the guns: a Remington 12-gauge pump-action shotgun with 14 rounds of 00-buckshot, an AR-15 Colt Sport Target Model .223-caliber with 15 rounds of ammunition, and 14 Smith & Wesson Model 67 .357 Magnum revolvers with 210 rounds of ammunition.

Halprin then placed a call to the maintenance department and told his accomplices that it was now safe to leave.

The other three inmates drove out of the maintenance garage and picked up Rivas, Halprin, Murphy, and the other inmate. Carrying the cache of weapons and ammunition taken from the guard tower, the group of escapees that would soon become known as the Texas 7 drove out of the prison's back gate in the white Texas Department of Criminal Justice truck, then down the perimeter road to freedom. They would launch one of the largest manhunts in U.S. history. And Some would compare their escape to the breakout at Alcatraz decades earlier.

As the investigation into the escape began, it was quickly discovered that the prisoners had left behind three notes. They wrote, in part, about the harshness of the Texas prison system and about creating a revolution within the Connally Unit. Another quoted a line from the Kris Kristofferson song, "Me and Bobby McGee" saying, "Freedom's just another word for nothin' left to lose." And in a third note they boldly stated, "You haven't heard the last of us yet. . . ."

CHAPTER

3

As Rivas, Murphy, Halprin, Rodriguez, Newbury, Garcia, and Harper were speeding down the perimeter road, correctional officer Lou Gips had managed to free himself and ran up the stairs to the top of the guard tower. From that vantage point, he could see the prisoners in the white truck, and he used his hand-held radio to request assistance. Gips reported that he was watching them drive past the 19 building, just outside of the compound, heading toward the road to town.

Warden Timothy B. Keith was on prison grounds with a police officer when he heard Gips's distress call over the radio. Not only was it a matter of grave concern, it was an embarrassment to have something like this occur in the presence of an outsider. On the other hand, the local police officer was able to quickly notify his colleagues to be on the lookout for a white Texas Department of Criminal Justice (TDCJ) truck. Warden Keith immediately ordered a lockdown.

Meanwhile, correctional officer Barton Olsen, assigned to oversee the community work squad, was on his way back to the prison when he heard one of the reports about the escape on his handheld radio. It was approximately two P.M., and the escapees had only been outside the prison compound for a few minutes when Olsen recalled seeing the white truck in downtown Kenedy, near City Hall. At the time he had merely thought prison employees were driving it on legitimate business, but after hearing the reports on his radio he realized it was the truck being sought. He immediately reported it. However, by the time the local police responded, the truck was already gone.

Within the hour every available law enforcement officer in the area was mobilized and on the lookout for the seven escapees. The Karnes County Sheriff's Department was brought in, as was the Texas Highway Patrol (Department of Public Safety). A white prison bus dropped every available prison officer 1,000 feet apart along Texas Highway 99, which runs northeast/southwest and connects to major interstates, to stand watch and help comb the area, which is punctuated by only an occasional home amid stands of barren trees. Motorists were stopped along every road that cut through this flat farmland area, identification was checked, and car trunks searched as motorists headed into or out of the area.

At approximately four P.M., as the intensive manhunt was underway, the white prison pickup was found abandoned behind a Wal-Mart store in Kenedy. The pickup was in the line of sight of a nearby automated teller machine located in the parking lot, and one of the investigators suggested that they take a look at the video footage it had recorded during the time frame in which they were interested, primarily between two and four.

After contacting the necessary bank official and obtaining a copy of the ATM videotape, investigators noted two vehicles that were present in the tape when the prison truck arrived but left the scene shortly afterward. The videotape was very poor and the images were difficult to discern, but one of the vehicles in question, a two-door compact car, appeared to be either a Chevrolet Cavalier or a Pontiac Sunbird, dark in color. Even though it was a very vague, general description, and despite the fact that it might not have even been the convicts' getaway car or cars, the information was circulated to police agencies throughout the state and was provided to the news media. No information about the possible second car was provided. Because there were no recent reports of stolen cars in the area, the investigators speculated that the inmates might have had outside help, someone who had dropped off the car or cars in the parking lot earlier that day. However, their trail seemed to vanish at the Kenedy Wal-Mart.

As darkness fell over this shocked and frightened community, authorities from around the state joined in the manhunt for the seven heavily armed escaped convicts.

"Everybody that we can get a hold of, every lawman in the State of Texas is looking for these guys," said Larry Todd, a spokesman for the TDCJ. "We certainly consider all of the inmates armed and dangerous. We know that they can become desperate . . . they may have split up, they may have gone in pairs. We don't know. What it tells us is that the escape appears to be well planned, from the inside of the unit to their arrival in the community." Todd stated that the investigators were looking into every possibility regarding any help that the escapees may have had, including possible help from friends and relatives.

That evening, the mood of Kenedy's citizenry remained tense, and many residents, particularly the elderly ones, were scared. Throughout the first night, authorities continued their search for the Texas 7 using hound dogs, helicopters, and all of the manpower that could be rounded up. An apartment complex near the Wal-Mart was searched, unit by unit, to make certain that the convicts had not taken anyone hostage and had not hidden inside an apartment. Despite the intensity of their efforts, no one was found. Law enforcement officers prepared themselves for what might turn out to be a long search effort.

"Right now, everything is at a standstill," said Robert Luna, a sergeant with the Bexar County Sheriff's Department. "We're still watching, but we're waiting for them to make a move."

"Right now we are combing the state for these people's relatives, their associates, their [former] places of employment, any place they frequented in the free world," said Glen Castlebury of the TDCJ. "They took people hostage, tied them up, and left them locked in a room. Put your stopwatch on it. By the time the front office declared, 'By God, it was an escape,' and sounded the alarm, they were gone. They were probably outside the perimeter before the perimeter was set up . . . We've got seven opportunities. Someone's gonna make a mistake, and if we get one of them, we may be on the road to catch all of them, even if they've broken up."

Although the cops didn't know it yet, the Texas 7 had spent their first night of freedom in San Antonio, a little over 60 miles up the road from Kenedy. They had likely taken the most direct route, U.S. 181, to get there.

By the following day, Thursday, December 14, authorities began to scale back their massive Karnes County search effort after conceding that the fugitives could be just about anywhere.

"We have no evidence that the men are in the area," Castlebury said of Thursday's dismantling of roadblocks and area search efforts. "We are effectively putting this in the hands of local and national

28

law enforcement agents." He indicated that the U.S. Marshals Service would be brought in to aid in the manhunt, as well as the Bureau of Alcohol, Tobacco, and Firearms.

The authorities also issued stern warnings to the convicts' family members, particularly two families in San Antonio, that they should not harbor the fugitives and should come forward if they had any information regarding their whereabouts.

"Things can be very bad for them if they don't," warned Karnes County Sheriff's Lieutenant Jim Rickhoff. "I would say the whole State of Texas is after these guys right now. They are extremely dangerous, very dangerous. This is certainly a huge community problem."

Meanwhile, incoming calls from concerned citizens claiming to have seen the fugitives began to flood already overworked staff at various law enforcement agencies. Officers dutifully followed up on the calls, but they had little or no substance. Nonetheless, they expressed their gratitude, realizing that it would be that "one" phone call that came in that would lead them to the fugitives. For the time being, updated bulletins were e-mailed and faxed to various city, county, state, and federal agencies, providing additional information on the escaped prisoners.

One of the things that troubled the authorities from the outset—aside from the fact that the inmates were serving long-term prison sentences on a variety of offenses that ranged from robbery to aggravated assault to rape to murder—was the fact that they had stolen wallets containing money, credit cards, and identification, all of which could aid them in staying out of sight.

Prison authorities were also troubled over the apparent ease with which the convicts escaped, prompting all kinds of speculation and questions regarding prison policies and procedures, and whether or not the inmates had any inside help. According to Castlebury, prison officials from outside the Connally Unit would conduct a complete review of the escape and the events that led up to it.

"Was the prison properly staffed, were procedures adhered to, were the inmates classified properly?" Castlebury said, referring to the types of questions that needed to be answered. "It's an extremely complicated review."

Despite the fact that each of the escaped inmates had been convicted of violent offenses, each had also earned minimum-security status due to good behavior. Although they were not allowed outside of the razor-wire–fenced areas, they were allowed the freedom to often go about the prison unsupervised.

As the search for the Texas 7 continued, the Connally Unit remained under lockdown for another day, and inmates were only allowed outside of their cells long enough to shower. The lockdown procedure would continue until prison officials were satisfied that there would not be an uprising and that there were no additional threats to security.

In the meantime, Castlebury remained optimistic that the seven escapees would be caught soon. He cited that out of 275 inmates who have escaped from Texas prisons over the past 16 years, only one has not been caught—a man who fled to Mexico, where there is no extradition treaty with the U.S.

"It may be a week, a month, or three months, but they're always back," Castlebury said.

CHAPTER
4

The Texas 7 did not remain in San Antonio for long. With their meager cash supply quickly running out, they left the city that is famous for the Alamo and Lackland Air Force Base and headed east toward Houston where, they hoped, they could replenish their funds by committing a holdup. George Rivas had a long history of armed robbery, and he patterned the latest one after those that had landed him in prison. They ended up at a Radio Shack in Pearland, a Houston suburb.

Newbury and Rivas had entered the store earlier in the day, and asked employee Michael Drab, 19, about lens caps for binoculars. They also asked to use the restroom, after which they left. However, the two of them returned just before closing time and announced to the employees and customers that they were there to rob the store. Drab, frightened over the ordeal, began to hyperventilate.

"Take deep breaths, Michael," Newbury said, reading Drab's name from his identification tag. "We're not here to hurt you . . . now, everyone empty out all of your pockets."

Newbury picked up the wallets, the money, and any change that had fallen onto the floor.

"Could you please give me my keys back?" asked one of the victims. "I need them for my work." Newbury agreed and handed the keys back to the man.

"How about my credit cards?" asked the same man. "Could I please have those back, too?" Newbury again agreed, and handed the man his credit cards. He handled them by their edges so that he would not leave fingerprints on them.

Meanwhile, Jim Drab, 53, a Pearland resident, was listening to the radio as he drove his van to the local Radio Shack, to pick up his son, Michael. As he pulled into the parking lot at about ten P.M. to wait for Michael, the last thing on his mind was that he might run into any of the escaped prisoners. But that is exactly what happened.

Rivas saw Drab park near the store, and asked the employees inside if anyone knew him. He was told that the man was Michael's father, picking him up from work.

Drab had just turned off the engine when he saw a

man, about 30, walking toward him. Drab rolled down the window to see what the man wanted. He didn't know that it was George Rivas, at least not at first.

"You here to pick up Michael?" asked the stranger, Rivas.

"Yes," Drab responded.

"Well, he's going to be a little late," Rivas said.

"Okay," Drab said, thinking that the man must be a new store employee sent out by his son. "I guess I can kill a little time and do some shopping." There were other stores nearby.

"Hey, would you mind buying me a Dr. Pepper? I'm really thirsty," Rivas asked, smiling. Drab looked at him quizzically but agreed as Rivas handed him four quarters. Rivas then turned and walked away from the van. However, before Drab could get out of his van and go into a nearby store, Rivas returned and leaned against the door of Drab's van. Rivas was carrying a cardboard box.

"I don't know how to tell you this," Rivas said, "but you caught us in the middle of a robbery." Rivas calmly opened the box he was carrying and displayed a handgun inside it to Drab. "Michael and the rest of the employees are in the back, tied up in the store. Nobody's going to get hurt as long as you do what I say."

Drab was stunned and at the same time frightened by Rivas's statement. He realized then that Rivas had approached him to buy a soda for him only to distract him from the robbery that was occurring, and to keep him busy for a couple of minutes. At first Drab considered faking a heart attack, or just speeding away, but decided against it because his son was being held hostage inside. He went into the store at Rivas's urging.

Donald Newbury was still with the four store employees and two customers they had rounded up, bound, and forced into the bathroom earlier. Rivas and Newbury had promised that they would not harm the frightened victims as long as they cooperated with them. The two convicts tied up Drab and forced him into the bathroom with the others. They made them all lie down on the floor. The escapees also took Drab's wallet, then proceeded to rob the store of thousands of dollars, walkie-talkies, other electronic equipment, and police scanners. Terrified, the victims did not know whether the robbers would return and shoot them or if they would merely leave. Fortunately, they took the stolen money and equipment and left the store.

"As things started to deteriorate, I started getting scared," Doug Watson, a store employee, later told the police and news media. "I wondered if I was going to get out of the situation. I was lucky enough not to be hurt."

"You'd expect them to be more desperate, mean and cruel," Drab said later, "but you would have them over for a barbecue if you didn't know they were crooks. That's how nice they were."

Nonetheless, Drab and Watson, as well as the others, later identified Rivas and Newbury from photos shown to them by the police, and the Pearland Radio Shack robbery would mark the first confirmed sighting of members of the Texas 7.

Drab and the cops didn't know it yet, but Rivas gave Drab's identification from his wallet to Larry Harper, who would begin using it from that day forward.

Following the Radio Shack robbery, the escaped convicts seemingly vanished into thin air. They were heading toward the Dallas-Fort Worth area while many in law enforcement figured that they would be heading south toward Mexico. The beefed-up security along the border between the U.S. and Mexico would ultimately be of no use in capturing the Texas 7.

As TDCJ officials began their investigation of the meticulously planned prison break, many began asking questions about the prison system's security lapses and whether or not the Texas 7 had inside help from a guard or supervisor. And many began to assess where blame for the escape might be laid. Low pay and understaffing at the prison, as well as throughout the system, was another issue after it was pointed out that correctional officers in Texas are among the lowest paid in the nation. Some people even tossed blame at former governor, and then president-elect of the U.S., George W. Bush for not doing anything about it, citing that the prison system had deteriorated to its present state under his watch. Even the classification system that categorized the seven escapees as "minimum security and [minimum] flight risks" came under fire. A complete investigation was ordered, and would be conducted by TDCJ officials outside the Connally Unit. The new Texas governor, Rick Perry, also ordered the Texas Rangers to join the investigation.

"Texas will spare no expense or energy in bringing those seven to justice," Perry said.

"The warden and the prison snitches are absolutely stunned that this large number of offenders could have pulled this off with no one else knowing," said Gary Johnson, the director of the TDCJ institutional division. "The events fit together like an intricate puzzle."

Meanwhile, prison officials began releasing information regarding prisoner escape and apprehension rates in an attempt to begin recovering from the embarrassment they felt after the brazen and seemingly easy escape from one of their maximum-security facilities. It was pointed out that Texas prisons have the lowest escape rate in the nation and the highest rate of apprehension. There were six escapes recorded in 1999, 16 in 1998, 16 again in 1997, and 22 in 1996. All were caught.

"We've always said that the average escapee remains free for only three hours and only gets three miles from the unit," said TDCJ spokesman Glen Castlebury. "Most of them don't get far enough to record them as escapes. It's a foolish thing to try, but they do it." Castlebury said that he did not know of any escapees who have caused serious bodily harm to anyone while on the run, and he hoped that the scenario would not change with the Texas 7, despite the fact that they had heavily armed themselves.

"A fleeing felon is a dangerous thing," said Castlebury.

Another issue that came up: The stiffer sentences being handed to offenders in recent years seemed to play a part in prompting more escapes and escape attempts. With three-strikes laws in place and tougher sentencing guidelines that turn into more life sentences without the possibility of parole, coupled with little chance at rehabilitation, many convicts figure that they have little to lose by making a break for freedom.

"Years ago, a lot of these men were looking at maybe 15-year sentences for their crimes," said a Texas prison official. "Nowadays, you've got young guys who won't be eligible for parole for 35 or 40 years. Some of these kids come in figuring, 'What do I have to lose?' Something clicks in their mind, 'I can't do this time.' "

By Sunday, December 17, the convicts were four days into their so-called freedom. The various law enforcement agencies were baffled as to their whereabouts, and despite the high volume of tips being called in, officials publicly admitted that they were not any closer to catching the convicts than they had been on the day of the escape. They issued requests for the public to keep an eye out for them but stressed that the seven men were dangerous criminals and none should be confronted.

"They are extremely dangerous," said TDCJ spokesman Larry Fitzgerald. "We urge the public at this time not to approach them." Fitzgerald said that the police were still looking for the dark, two-door compact car, either a Cavalier or a Sunbird, and asked the public to report any sightings of such cars.

In an attempt to further educate the public as well as other law enforcement agencies around the country about the Texas 7, Texas officials placed photos and criminal histories of each of the escapees on the official TDCJ Web site under a "fugitive watch" link. The FBI soon joined the other agencies in the manhunt, and placed similar information about the escapees on its official Web site as well.

Because of reported sightings of the convicts in and around San Antonio, and prior to it being known that they had moved on to the Houston area, a task force comprised of some two dozen sheriff's deputies and U.S. marshals had been set up in outlying Bexar County near San Antonio. At least two of the convicts, both convicted murderers, had close relatives living in the San Antonio area, whom investigators remained in close contact with just in case the fugitives attempted to get in touch with them to ask for assistance. Nothing.

And later, despite the efforts of all the agencies involved, there were no solid leads as to where the fugitives might have gone after the Radio Shack robbery in Pearland.

"We think they're hunkered down somewhere," said TDCJ spokesman Larry Todd. "They can't stay there forever. The fugitives will be captured. It's just a matter of time."

Unknown to the investigators, the Texas 7 were lying low in Farmers Branch, a Dallas-Fort Worth suburb near Irving, Texas. On Tuesday, December 19, four of the fugitives checked into an Econo Lodge under an assumed name. Frugal spenders, upon check-in they used a coupon for a discount rate for their first night's stay and reserved the room for the coming week. They paid in cash and lied to the desk clerk that only four men would be staying in the room; otherwise they would have been required to rent two rooms. The desk clerk issued them a room on the ground floor next door to the motel's assistant manager. Although it was the motel's usual policy to photocopy each guest's driver's license or identification card, that didn't happen in this case. The desk clerk did record the license number of the vehicle they were driving—an older Chevrolet Suburban, and not a Cavalier or Sunbird like the one the authorities were looking for. Because the motel's employees had no idea that they were dealing with the escaped convicts, it would be some time before that information was turned over to the police.

In the meantime the Texas 7 were moving about when necessary, hiding in plain sight while plotting their next move.

CHAPTER

5

In the days before Christmas, details about the backgrounds of the seven convicts on the run began to emerge. As their faces became more frighteningly familiar to the general public, so did the information about their criminal histories. One was sentenced to prison for severely beating an infant, another was convicted of being a serial rapist, another for raping a former high school classmate, one for armed robbery, one for burglary, and two for calculated, cold-blooded murder.

Patrick Henry Murphy, Jr., was born in Dallas, Texas, on October 31, 1961, making him 39 years old at the time of his escape from the John Connally Unit. The former construction worker had done a stint in the U.S. Army but was dishonorably discharged due to the fact that he kept going AWOL. Although he had occasionally gotten into trouble while growing up in the Dallas area, it was difficult to picture, at least in 1978, the skinny high school boy with the Beatles haircut and the peach-fuzz mustache as a rapist. To those who knew him he just seemed like a normal, occasionally mischievous sophomore. But by 1984 that is exactly what the brown-haired, blue-eyed young man had become: a rapist.

He had first become known to the law enforcement community as a professional burglar, for which he was originally arrested. However, after agreeing to testify against another man, he was sentenced to probation.

Slightly built at 5'7" tall and weighing in at less than 160 pounds. Murphy did not appear to be the rapist type, if there is, in fact, such a "type." But that's what he did on a night in 1984, to a 23-year-old divorced woman that he knew from high school and who was living with her mother.

It began as a simple burglary. However, it turned ugly when the young woman was awakened by a noise. When she got up to investigate, she saw a man in the living room of her mother's home. His face was covered. When Murphy realized that he had been seen, he grabbed the woman and held a knife to her throat.

"Keep your eyes shut and be quiet, or something might happen," Murphy said.

Fearing for her life, the young woman submitted to Murphy's demands and allowed him to cover her head with a pillowcase. He then cut off her nightgown with the knife and raped her. Afterward, when she was certain that her assailant had left the premises, the young woman woke up her mother and tearfully told her that she had been raped.

They called the police and reported the attack, and the woman assured the police that she would recognize her assailant's voice if she heard it again. She thought she knew the man's voice and was able to eventually put the cops onto Murphy. After his arrest, she positively identified his voice from a "voice lineup."

At his trial, a jury was carefully questioned about whether they could make a fair judgment based on voice identification. When all parties were satisfied and a jury was seated, tearful testimony from the victim was presented as she explained the burglary and subsequent rape. Afterward, jurors only deliberated for a few hours before convicting Murphy of aggravated sexual assault with a deadly weapon and burglary. The judge sentenced him to 50 years in prison.

Murphy promptly appealed his sentence in the form of a neatly written letter of protest to the judge:

"I respectfully request to appear in your court to personally voice my request to reduce my sentence of 50 years to a substantially lower sentence," Murphy wrote. "My reasons for reduction of sentence are rather lengthy, but will not take long to present to you in court."

The judge denied Murphy's request and subsequent appeals, and he served the next 16 years in prison. Before the December 13 breakout, Murphy had 15 months to go before becoming eligible for parole.

Following the escape, Murphy's half sister, Kristina Rogers, told the news media that Murphy had appeared remorseful for his crimes the last time she had talked to him. She said he had been making plans to open up a woodworking shop when he got out of prison. Kristina, along with Michael Murphy, one of Patrick's uncles, made a futile appeal to Murphy via a television news program to surrender. Afterward, an FBI wanted poster showed older photos of Murphy, one with a beard and one without, as well as an artist's rendering of how he might look at the present time. The FBI described Murphy as having a scar on his abdomen and a burn scar on his right forearm.

The fact that he had used a pillowcase to cover his victim's head was immediately familiar, and prompted the investigators probing the prison break to speculate that the pillowcases used in the escape to cover those victims' faces may have been Murphy's touch.

Donald Keith Newbury, 38, was born on May 18, 1962, in Albuquerque, New Mexico. Although there are no apparent arrest records there for Newbury, he was a three-time felon before the jail break, with a criminal record in Texas that dated back to 1981. Among the seven escapees, Newbury had the longest rap sheet.

According to court records, Newbury first went to prison for an armed robbery he committed in Austin, Texas, in 1981. After serving only a few years he was paroled, but he was convicted of armed robbery a second time in 1987, also in Austin. He was the prime suspect in approximately 12 other armed robberies there in 1986 and 1987. Three of those in which he was a suspect included attacks on hotels, another involved the robbery of a cabdriver, two were committed at surplus stores, and another involved a Trailways bus.

Following his release from his second prison term in the early 1990s, Newbury met a woman who lived in a rural area outside Austin, and moved in with her and her two children. At that time, according to acquaintances, it appeared that Newbury was making an effort to go straight. He urged his girlfriend and her children to stay out of trouble and was known to refer to a movie, *American Me*, that depicts prison life. He was always telling his girlfriend and her kids that that's what it is like in prison, and urged them not to ever do anything that would cause them to end up behind bars.

Despite his efforts, he had a tough time finding work as an ex-con in the small town where he lived and ended up working as a laborer for an ex-felon, a direct violation of parole regulations that prohibit parolees from associating with other ex-convicts. He was eventually brought in on the violation.

"His parole officer from that area testified on his behalf as to basically how difficult it was to make it in a rural area when you're on parole," said his attorney, Kent Anschutz. "It's hard enough to get work as a parolee in a big city, probably double that in a small town . . . I'd say he's average or above-average intelligence. He struck me as actually a pretty likable old boy who had made some bad decisions."

In addition to being likable and good to the woman and children he was living with, Newbury was not known to drink or to do drugs. However, no matter how hard he tried, Newbury apparently could not refrain from making those bad decisions. On July 18, 1997, Newbury, wielding a sawed-off shotgun, walked into a La Quinta Inn just off Interstate 35 in Austin and robbed the desk clerk of $65 cash. That robbery, along with a string of other robberies he was suspected of committing along I-35, earned him the moniker "the I-35 Robber."

"You were lucky," Newbury told the clerk as he turned and ran out.

The police obtained a surveillance tape from the hotel's management and released segments to the public. It didn't take long for the police to close in and capture him.

"He was almost a likable guy," said Austin Police Sergeant Mark Balagia, who helped capture Newbury for the I-35 robberies, "if you didn't think about what he had done."

"I think he has no problem holding up sawed-off shotguns to people and taking their money," said the lead prosecutor in Newbury's 1997 trial. The judge apparently agreed and, reviewing his past criminal record, sentenced him to 99 years in prison after classifying him as a habitual criminal, despite the fact that a former parole officer testified in his behalf.

"The officer was fairly sympathetic to him and, I believe, felt that he had tried real hard while he was on parole," said Anschutz. "It's not every day that a person in the criminal justice system would say anything positive about an individual under their charge."

According to TDCJ records, Newbury stated that he does not need to use drugs, alcohol, or even smoke cigarettes because "the adrenaline rush he receives from his robberies is what he lives for."

At the time of his escape from the Connally Unit, Newbury was described as a 6' 1", 202-pound white man with brown hair and eyes. He had identifying scars on the top of his right knee, another under his left eye, and a scar from a medical procedure on the outside of his right elbow. He also had tattoos all over his body, including on his neck, and a distinctive tattoo of a lizard on his upper left arm.

Joseph C. Garcia, 29 at the time of his escape, was born in San Antonio, Texas, on November 6, 1971, to a middle class family. According to court records, the 5'11" 198-pound Garcia had not been in serious trouble with the law and had only a few misdemeanor arrests until February 1996. At that time the brown-haired, brown-eyed young man was only 24, and was married to a young woman.

Garcia, who had been employed as a maintenance worker at a San Antonio airport hangar, had a penchant for drinking after work and on his days off. On a chilly February night in 1996 Garcia, Miguel Luna, and another friend were on their way home after spending much of the day in a bar, drinking. Garcia was going to drop Luna off first, but Luna provided incorrect directions to his home and Garcia became lost in San Antonio. In their drunken state of mind, Garcia and Luna began arguing over the terrible directions.

Soon the argument escalated to a physical altercation. Garcia pulled over and stopped the car, after which Luna attacked Garcia, grabbed the car keys and ran off down the street. Garcia chased after Luna and pulled out a knife while he was running. When he caught up with Luna and tackled him in the courtyard of an apartment complex, he began stabbing him with the knife, repeatedly, according to witnesses.

"Die, motherfucker, die!" Garcia yelled as he continued to stab Luna.

A short time later Luna did just that, from the 19 stab wounds that Garcia had inflicted upon him, 16 of which were to Luna's chest and back. Garcia was subsequently arrested and charged with Luna's murder. He claimed he killed Luna in self-defense.

"He continued to mad-dog me, which is to constantly look at me just in an ugly way," Garcia testified at his trial. "I had the feeling that Miguel wanted to fight. And I don't fight. As a matter of fact, I have never fought in my life."

"Mike Luna will never go home again," argued the prosecutor at the trial. "These three babies," he said, referring to Luna's three daughters, "will never have a reason to make Father's Day gifts for their dad. These three little girls can never, ever expect gifts under their Christmas tree from their daddy."

The jury convicted Garcia of Luna's murder, and the judge handed him a 50-year sentence in prison.

While serving that sentence at the Connally Unit, Garcia wrote a number of letters and motions complaining to the judge that his court-appointed attorney had not been provided the necessary time to prepare a proper defense.

"I am not stupid, nor is my family," Garcia wrote. "We might be a middle-class people, but we are a smart middle-class people."

The judge apparently did not agree with him and denied his motions for a new trial.

At the time of his escape, Garcia was described as appearing thinner than in his mug shots, with longer hair. He had tattoos of a yin and yang symbol on his right back shoulder, a scar on his left thigh, a surgery scar on the left side of his groin area, and the name

ARLENE tattooed on his right wrist. He also wore thick, black-framed glasses and a black onyx ring.

Randy Ethan Halprin, 23 years old at the time of his escape from prison, was born to abusive parents in McKinney, Texas, on September 13, 1977. Randy and his younger brother, Wesley, were removed from their abusive home by the Child Protective Services in 1983 and were temporarily placed in foster homes. A short time later Daniel and Patricia Halprin, a kind-hearted couple from Dalworthington Gardens, who owned an electronics business, adopted the two boys, gave them their surname, and took them into their comfortable home.

"They came out of Child Protective Services cases that were pretty difficult," said Dalworthington Gardens Police Chief Bill Waybourn, who is also a family friend of the Halprins. "They came out of a pretty abusive home."

According to Waybourn, Halprin was an intelligent youngster. By the time he was 13, however, he began having problems with reality.

"One of the most significant [problems]," Waybourn said, "was that he thought aliens were going to be landing. He took maps, marked landing sites, and so forth . . . he wasn't unintelligent. He could form a plan and execute it."

On one occasion Halprin went on a camp outing with his church near Lake Worth. A sign of his antisocial behavior reared its head during the outing when Halprin managed to persuade 30 other boys to sneak out of the camp with him at night. He ended up leading them into Fort Worth, several miles away.

Waybourn, who had been friends with the Halprin family for more than a decade, took it upon himself at one point to try and counsel young Randy. Waybourn had been a security police officer while serving in the U.S. Air Force, and Randy had indicated to him that he wanted to follow in his footsteps. However, Halprin didn't have what it takes, at least not behaviorally.

As his behavior continued to slide downward, his adoptive parents took action and sent him to a boarding school in Kentucky. At first Randy was not a disciplinary problem at the school. And he maintained good grades, at least for a while. However, that all changed rather quickly, according to the school's dean.

"Randy didn't seem to be a bad kid," said the dean. "His grades were mostly above average. He got into trouble for being in the girls' bathroom with a girl once. He sneaked out of his dorm once by tying sheets together and climbing out, when he could have just as easily walked out the front door.

"But he got worse," continued the dean. "Over Christmas 1995, he went and stayed at the home of another student in Lexington and did some shoplifting. He was put on school probation, and then carved his name and some girl's name into some brand-new wooden benches here. I expelled him, and his father said he couldn't come home. He was through with him."

According to the dean, Halprin moved into the home of a student who did not live on campus and was later permitted to return to school. However, he was soon caught stealing from a student's home and then decided to move away and leave school on his own.

After leaving the boarding school, Halprin's adoptive parents decided to help him get an apartment in Kentucky and to assist him financially.

"His parents paid for an apartment for him," said Waybourn, "but he cashed it in, took the money and began living on the streets and off the system. Living in homeless shelters, that's how he fed and clothed himself."

Halprin eventually returned to Texas and began staying at a homeless shelter in Fort Worth. While there he met a woman with an infant and befriended her. They soon became acquainted with some other people, pooled what little money they were able to get their hands on, and together they all moved out of the shelter and into an apartment on Fort Worth's west side. The move would ultimately become the beginning of the end for Halprin's life as a free man.

When Halprin met the woman at the homeless shelter, he hadn't given any thought as to whether he liked children or not. He soon found out that he didn't. On a day in August 1996, the woman's baby began crying and would not stop. The child soon got on Halprin's nerves.

Since talking to the infant did no good, Halprin repeatedly beat and kicked the boy. When the paramedics examined the child, they discovered, much to their horror, that his arms and legs were broken, he had multiple skull fractures, a black eye, and a ruptured eardrum.

After Halprin was arrested, he was examined by a court-appointed psychiatrist who found that he demonstrated average intelligence but had "major" problems with impulse control.

"Couple this with poor judgment and a tremendous problem arises," the psychiatrist wrote in a report for the court.

"He brutalized that baby pretty badly," Waybourn said. "When that episode happened, I went, 'Ooh.' I knew he was having some issues, but I didn't think he'd get violent."

Facing serious charges against him, Halprin pleaded guilty to causing serious bodily injury to a child. A judge sentenced him to 30 years in prison.

"I know Randy came from a bad environment," said Waybourn. "But a lot of other people come from bad environments and don't make the kind of choices he did. Randy made his own choices, and they were bad. Now, he's made another one."

Larry James Harper was 37 years old when he broke out of the Connally Unit. He was serving a 50-year sentence for a string of rapes he committed in the early 1990s. Born in Danville, Illinois, on September 10, 1963, the 5'11" 165-pound man with black hair and brown eyes always seemed mild-mannered and was always well groomed.

Harper, a former honor student, tried hard to follow in the footsteps of his father, who he rarely saw, a highly decorated command sergeant major who served in the army's Special Forces in Vietnam.

"He had a chest-and-a-half full of medals when I saw him last," said Harper's attorney, Charles Roberts.

Despite earning an associate's degree in military science from the private Kemper Military School in Boonville, Missouri, joining the Army Reserve, going through airborne and infantry training, and informally participating in Green Beret training exercises, Harper fell short of the expectations that he had set for himself and he often expressed disappointment at not being able to follow his father's lead.

According to court testimony, Harper's mother, a native of Korea, was a former prostitute his father met in a bar in that country. Having been sexually abused during the Korean War, she was said to have beaten Harper and his brother repeatedly.

"Apparently, that brutalization was passed on to Harper and his brother," Roberts said. "In one case, the dad . . . was recalled from Vietnam because the situation had gotten so bad with his children."

"We were a family hiding and ducking from each

other," Harper's brother would later say.

Harper's mother divorced his father when Harper was ten and completely severed ties with her family. As a result, Harper and his brother ended up living with their father on military bases. Despite the fact that the boys lived with their father, he had little time to spend with them, according to Karen Gold, a psychiatrist who evaluated Harper prior to his going to prison.

"His father was quite committed to his own military career and was not all that available," Gold said. "[Larry Harper] was plagued by issues having to do with being abandoned and not having much of a sense of self-worth."

Despite his issues, Harper attended the University of Texas at El Paso in 1986 and majored in marketing. According to university records, he continued his studies until 1994. In addition to being a full-time student, he worked as a substitute teacher and held a part-time job as a bookstore clerk. At the time he committed his offenses, he was an honor student. Up until that time, he had never been in trouble with the law. According to Dr. Gold, it was in the latter half of 1993 that Harper broke up with a girlfriend and began drinking heavily. At about that time a string of rapes began near the university campus. According to court records, Harper's first known rape offense occurred on September 3, 1993.

"I'm not going to let you go to waste," Harper told

his female victim as he held a knife on her. He then raped her.

A little more than a month later, on October 5, he committed another rape. In that particular case he bound his female victim and sexually assaulted her in a number of different ways and left a pair of scissors next to her when he was finished.

"Don't cut yourself free for a few minutes," he warned his victim as he left.

On October 31, Halloween night, as well as on the following night, he was caught in an act of voyeurism as he peeped into windows at two women, in two different apartments, at an apartment complex near the campus. When confronted by a security guard during the November 1 incident, Harper was found to be carrying a screwdriver, a pair of scissors, and two rolls of electrical tape. It was generally believed later that, if not caught peeping on those two occasions, he would have raped those women, too. He escaped going to jail that time.

"He was amazed he got away with it," Gold said. "He was filled with remorse—very, very ashamed of himself. But for a few short spaces in time, he felt he was in control rather than being controlled."

Four nights later, on November 4, according to court records, he was observed peeping into yet another woman's window and was caught unscrewing a lightbulb on her porch. Again, he was not prosecuted. Four months later, on March 23, 1994, he returned to the woman's apartment where he had been peeping on the previous October 31 and raped her. It became the incident for which he would be arrested and would eventually connect him to the other rapes and crimes of voyeurism.

"He had nothing but rejection from women," Dr. Gold said. "He's one sick puppy . . . not the usual jail inmate, the kind who is cocky and proud of his crimes. He is extremely depressed. It is chronic, serious depression." She also described him as "smart and disciplined."

Dr. Gold also said she believed he had suicidal tendencies.

"If it's possible for Mr. Harper to step in front of a peace officer and point a gun at him and commit suicide by cop, that's very likely what he'll do," Gold said reflecting on his case, following his breakout from the Connally Unit.

Unlike many criminals, Harper did not dispute his actions and pleaded guilty to them. He apologized repeatedly to his victims and took full responsibility for his crimes. He seemed sincerely remorseful.

"I acted in a weak and cowardly manner," Harper told the court. "I am to be blamed for what I have done."

Even though the case did not go to trial, a jury was impaneled to hear the details of the case and decide his sentence. His father testified on his behalf and said that he was aware of the abuse and expressed sorrow that his military career had prevented him from stopping it. Afterward, the jury sentenced Harper to 50 years in prison.

"I still have hopes that . . . after leaving prison, he simply walked away [from the others]," Roberts said after the break. "I just think that the sentence was unbearable. That's why he may have gone along with these people."

Michael Anthony Rodriguez, 38, was born in San Antonio, Texas, on October 29, 1962. Like Joseph Garcia, he still had ties there following his escape from the Connally Unit, and both men were convicted murderers, but that was as far as the similarities between the two men went. While Garcia worked and lived as a blue-collar laborer and drank cheap beer in less than desirable bars, Rodriguez ran his own restaurant, dressed fashionably, wore a Rolex, and drove around town in his yellow classic Mercedes-Benz. As a youth, he attended the private Central Catholic High School in San Antonio, and was always looking toward the future. Ironically, the detective who investigated the murder of Rodriguez's wife and helped send Rodriguez to prison was an old classmate from Central Catholic.

While still in his twenties, Rodriguez worked at a local Taco Bell fast-food restaurant and saved his money diligently to put toward his dream: opening his own Mexican restaurant someday. After saving $9,000, he asked his father, Raul Rodriguez, for a $15,000 loan to go with what he had saved. His father, who owned a convenience store, wanted to see his son succeed and he agreed to loan him the money for the restaurant. As a result, Rodriguez soon opened the Taco House Restaurant, and it became an almost instant success. By 1992, Rodriguez and his wife, Theresa, were living well. It was at about that time that Rodriguez decided that he wanted to become a teacher, and he began taking courses in education at Southwest Texas State University in San Marcos.

While attending classes, a young woman caught Rodriguez's eye and he began writing letters to her expressing his affection. He described himself to the young woman as a lonely widower. To others, particularly his brother Mark, he had complained how his wife had gotten fat after they were married and he began exploring ways to get rid of her. With Mark's help, he began to explore another option: murder.

Mark was a cocaine dealer at the lower end of the drug-trafficking spectrum, and he always seemed to be in need of money. Theresa, 30, was more than adequately insured, with two $150,000 life insurance policies in her name listing her husband as the beneficiary. Before long the two brothers began to conspire to kill Theresa. Mark assured Michael he could find a killer and that he would do so for a $50,000 cut of the insurance money. He said he would use the money to expand his cocaine trade.

"Mark was kind of the brains of the whole thing," said Detective Sergeant Andy Hernandez of the San Antonio Police Department. "Michael is a follower.

He's influenced very easily. Mark is the one who put him up to it."

The two brothers found Roland Ruiz, 20, an ex-con who had just gotten out of jail on robbery charges. Ruiz needed money, so he agreed to kill Theresa for $2,000.

The plan called for Michael and Theresa to drive to Macaroni's Restaurant, where Ruiz would be waiting. He would shoot Theresa in the parking lot as she and Michael arrived for dinner. However, Ruiz backed out at the last minute. There were security guards on the premises, which he had not expected. After their plans went awry several more times, the three men finally decided to commit the murder at Rodriguez's home. It would be done at night, when Michael and Theresa returned home from an outing.

It was on an evening in October 1992 when the plot was finally brought to fruition. Michael and Theresa had gone out to the movies. As Rodriguez was pulling the Mercedes into the garage, Ruiz ran up to the passenger side of the car and shot Theresa one time in the head as she opened the car door to get out. Ruiz fled afterward, and Theresa died almost instantly.

Ruiz's mother, suspicious because of all the new clothing and other items he was buying, knew that her son had been up to no good and kicked him out of the house. Soon his money was gone too.

The police were onto the three men within days. They learned, among other things, that Rodriguez had gone out drinking with friends on the night of his wife's funeral. They also learned about the letters that he had written to the young woman at the university, claiming to be a widower before the fact. And then they learned about Ruiz, who broke down and confessed after being confronted about Theresa's murder.

"I spent all of it on clothes and partying," Ruiz would later tell the police. "I bought a lot of clothes at Dillard's and Foley's. My mother got suspicious of me having all of this money. She threw me out of the house."

Ruiz told the police that Theresa had barely opened the car door when he ran up and shot her.

"She looked at me and smiled," Ruiz said.

After being confronted by the police with Ruiz's statement, Michael Rodriguez confessed to his part in the plot to murder his wife.

Michael Rodriguez, along with his brother, Mark, received life sentences for Theresa's murder. Roland Ruiz received the death penalty.

George Rivas, 30, also known as George Angel Rivas, George Angel Potter, Angel George Potter, and George Potter, was a career criminal. Highly intelligent with a larger than life ego, it is little wonder that he plotted the Connally Unit breakout and appointed himself ringleader of the Texas 7. When it comes time for him to leave this world, an appropriate epitaph might read, "Convicted of crimes against humanity, and guilty of a wasted life."

Born in El Paso, Texas, on May 6, 1970, the six-foot, 231-pound brown-haired, brown-eyed criminal with rugged good looks and a soft-spoken voice could have been just about anything he wanted to make of himself, had it not been for his lust for cash.

Rivas, described by a former classmate as a "Beavis and Butt-Head kind of guy," had aspirations of becoming a policeman before he turned to a life of crime, and he spoke of his dream often. But he would never become a cop. Raised by his grandmother and grandfather after his parents divorced when he was six, Rivas cruised through high school without attracting a lot of attention. Having a fascination with guns, he named his two dogs Ruger and Beretta, and began thinking about a life of crime.

Characterized as intelligent, well spoken, and friendly, Rivas did not get into trouble with the law until shortly after graduating from Ysleta High School in 1988 where, according to a high school spokesman, he was identified as a quiet guy who did not participate in any school activities. He committed his first robbery and burglary the following year, but since he had no prior criminal record he was sentenced to probation for ten years.

While on probation, Rivas enrolled at the University of Texas at El Paso where he signed up as a general studies major in the fall of 1992. After three semesters, unable to shake his criminal bent and lust for cash, he dropped out in the spring of 1993 and embarked on a short-lived criminal career that would land him in prison. There were striking similarities between his earlier crimes, which tied him to a string of robberies in El Paso, and the prison breakout and the robbery of the Radio Shack in Pearland. A similar modus operandi was also on display during a string of holdups, at least a dozen, that he was suspected of committing in Texas, New Mexico, and Arizona.

One of the robberies he was suspected of committing occurred on October 3, 1992, at a Radio Shack in El Paso. According to a police report, he was suspected of handcuffing a salesman and then robbing the store of cash, two-way radios, as well as other merchandise.

Less than three weeks later, on October 23, he was suspected of entering a Checker Auto Parts store under the guise of buying a car battery when he pulled a gun on a salesman. He was accused of forcing the salesman to remove his store shirt, after which he handcuffed him and forced him into the restroom. He then put on the shirt and forced the store's assistant manager to open the safe, and he cleaned out all the cash on hand.

Barely two weeks after the auto parts store robbery, Rivas walked into an El Paso Oshman's Sporting Goods store near closing time, under the guise of looking at ski boots. He went so far as to ask the assistant manager to keep the store open a bit longer so that he could purchase a pair of the boots, and explained that he was waiting for a friend to bring his wallet to him. When he was satisfied that he had the assistant manager's cooperation, he pulled out a gun and ordered him to call all of the employees together, then announced, "This is a robbery." He then called an accomplice on a two-way radio, took a store shirt from an employee and put it on so that he wouldn't unduly stand out, just in case someone, say the police unexpectedly came in, and he and his accomplice handcuffed all of the employees except one to a heavy ski grinding machine. Afterward, Rivas forced the store's manager to empty the safe for him. He took all of the cash, $5,095, as well as 58 guns. He didn't touch anything during the robbery, but instead forced the employee to pick up and pack the items that he wanted to steal.

"I've written down all of your license plate numbers and can find out where you live if anyone tries to identify us," Rivas said as he and his accomplice left the store. He also said that he would return and kill them if anyone called the police.

The employees waited about 20 minutes after Rivas and his accomplice left the store. They then dragged the ski grinding machine to a phone and called the police, after which they dragged the machine back to its original location out of fear that Rivas might return and find out what they had done.

His next known robbery occurred on May 12, 1993, when, donning a blond wig and brandishing a gun, he went inside a Furr's grocery store in El Paso and forced all of the employees into a back room. He took all of the cash that he could locate.

On May 25, 1993, Rivas and an accomplice disguised themselves as security guards and walked into a Toys 'R' Us store. After rounding up eight employees, Rivas and his accomplice robbed the establishment. Although his previous robberies had been carried out with military precision, in this case he somehow missed one of the employees, who escaped and called the police. When the police arrived, Rivas and his accomplice held them at bay for more than three hours by using the employees as hostages. However, a SWAT team was called in when the police officers realized that they weren't going to get anywhere. The SWAT team stormed the store and found Rivas, wearing a blond wig, hiding in an air conditioning duct. They also recovered some of the guns that had been stolen from the Oshman's Sporting Goods store robbery earlier. Although his arrest ended the string of local robberies, he was still suspected of committing the numerous robberies in other parts of Texas, Arizona, and New Mexico.

Following his arrest, numerous employees from the various stores he had robbed positively identified Rivas as the perpetrator. At his trial, he claimed he was having dinner with his wife during the Oshman's robbery and had been mistakenly identified. The jury didn't buy his claims of mistaken identity in that case, or any of the others, and he was convicted of multiple counts of aggravated armed robbery, aggravated kidnapping, and burglary, *under various theories of law.*

"He was still making plans on how they were going

to escape," one of the prosecutors said regarding the Toys 'R' Us robbery. "They were under siege, and he was still trying to keep his ring together." One of the other prosecutors characterized Rivas as "having a lot of gall."

"He is very strong and dominant with a conceited and arrogant personality," said one of his codefendants in the Oshman's and Toys 'R' Us holdups. "He considers himself a master criminal mind and a leader among men."

Dr. Richard Coons, a court-appointed Austin psychiatrist, examined Rivas prior to his trial. Despite the fact that nobody had been injured during the commission of any of Rivas's crimes, Coons opinion was that had only been a matter of luck and not because of Rivas's kindness.

"He demonstrates an unusual degree of interest, creativity, and intensity in his craft," Coons said. "He is confident and arrogant. He is a mastermind and a leader. He has no conscience, and he does not speak the truth."

Rivas was sentenced to 18 life terms in prison, 17 of which were ordered to run consecutively. The judge wanted to make certain that he never left prison alive.

Following his escape from the Connally Unit, Dr. Coons was contacted by members of the news media and related that when Rivas and his cohorts were found and confronted by the police, the confrontation would likely turn deadly.

"If anybody had got in his way, he would have shot them," Coons said of Rivas's prison escape. "The odds are it will be a shootout with hostages [when confronted]. I would advise the police not to try to take them if it's a hostage situation. There will be a lot of bodies."

CHAPTER

6

More than a week after the Texas 7 broke out of the Connally Unit, authorities were no closer to catching the fugitives who had launched the largest manhunt in modern Texas history. Law enforcement officials claimed that the level of planning that went into the breakout would have taken months, and it was generally agreed upon that it would have taken several weeks for the prisoners to collect and carefully hide nine pillowcases and a sheet, and to make and hide the shanks and other weapons they used. Even as the massive manhunt was underway, Texas officials were still looking for somewhere to lay the blame for the daring escape.

One of the problems that made the escape possible,

according to prison officials, was prison security it-self. The security measures that were in place at the Connally Unit had been set up for the more traditional types of escape attempts, like the desperate convict who tries to go over a fence when he thinks no one is looking. The Connally Unit wasn't prepared for an elaborate escape scheme planned by smarter-than-average prisoners.

"The unit's escape plans were designed for a conventional escape," said Johnny Vasquez, Jr., 38, a former prison official who previously supervised the prison's security plans and left his job in October 2000 so that he could begin training as a police officer. "You know these guys are in a vehicle, you know that in five minutes they're five miles away. It did almost no good to put officers along the road and in the checkpoints around the prison."

"What does a warden at a prison have?" asked TDCJ spokesman Glen Castlebury, in defense of the prison officials' actions following the escape. "Dogs and horses. They do perimeter searches . . . you ain't going to send any of our correctional officers out on the highways chasing fugitives. That's what DPS [Department of Public Safety] and the sheriff's departments are for." Castlebury said that as prison officials were conducting the perimeter search in the hours following the escape, bulletins were being sent to law enforcement agencies from South Texas to the Mexican border and across the nation.

One of the problems that may have facilitated the

escape, according to Vasquez, was that the seven inmates did not show up for lunch at the mess hall and their absence went unnoticed by the correctional officers on duty. Vasquez said that their absence from the 11:15 A.M. lunch should have raised flags, and because they went unnoticed they had more than two hours to carry out their carefully laid out plan. According to Vasquez, who worked at the Connally Unit for two and a half years and was an 11-year veteran of the prison system, this kind of lax security is present throughout the entire Texas prison system. It should have been questioned whether or not such hardcore criminals should have such liberties in a maximum-security setting.

"This was something that was brewing," Vasquez said. "Instead of being concerned with security as a priority, other areas were being given priority, such as getting nationally accredited. The focus was on making sure the walls were clean and the floors were scrubbed, yet inmates were running up and down the hallways."

Photos of inside the prison after the break illustrated the cleanliness. For a correctional institution, the Connally Unit appeared immaculately clean despite the fact that the prison was inadequately staffed and the employees underpaid. At the time of the prison breakout, the Connally Unit was short by nearly 80 guards, and the shift during which the breakout occurred was short 33 guards. Nonetheless, prison officials were adamant that the staff shortages could not be blamed for the escape.

According to Castlebury, the inmates were never unsupervised and they were not in violation of any of the prison's rules by not eating their lunch in the mess hall. They did notify their supervisors that they were taking their lunch in the maintenance department, he said.

"If they chose not to go down and eat our food, that's their business," Castlebury said. "They gathered around a work bench inside the maintenance shop inside the secure premises of the prison." Castlebury said that the inmates were serving their lengthy sentences in a minimum-custody situation because they had earned it due to good behavior. Their good behaviors had also earned them commissary privileges and, because of that, they were allowed to eat outside the dining hall provided that they were under supervision.

The classification system that is used to assign prisoners jobs and housing is another problem that needs to be addressed, according to Vasquez. Instead of basing such assignments on the security risk a given inmate poses, those assignments are sometimes made on the importance of an inmate's job skills.

"The needs of the institution sometimes superseded the inmate's behavior or their record," Vasquez said. "It doesn't matter that they're murderers if they've got the skills." Vasquez added that six out of the seven escapees worked in the maintenance department, among the most sensitive areas of the prison. "Maintenance has access to the floor plans. They know which keys go to which doors, they know all the heating and ventilation systems, they know absolutely every inch of that facility. They know where everything is at . . . these guys knew the weaknesses in the system, they knew the time when they could do it. It's embarrassing, really."

Despite the fact that informal relationships between the prison staff and inmates is strictly forbidden by the prison system's regulations, it was not all that uncommon for a supervisor to ask advice of an inmate in order to find a qualified worker for the maintenance crew. George Rivas, in his position as a maintenance department clerk, would have been able to handpick the inmates he wanted. According to a top-level prison official who talked to the news media but did not want to be identified, that's how Rivas might have been able to get the guys he wanted to involve in his escape plans, by manipulating a supervisor.

It was generally believed that Rivas had been able to earn the loyalty of five of the other six inmates by helping them obtain work assignments in the maintenance department, considered one of the best job assignments for inmates. The exception would have been Rodriguez, who was assigned to the outside yard crew. The loyalty factor to Rivas may have held them together after the escape, as opposed to their breaking up and going their own separate ways.

In the aftermath of the Connally Unit breakout,

prison officials from around the state began assessing security issues at other state prisons to help ensure that such an escape did not occur at another facility.

"We checked all of our procedures," said James Duke, senior warden at the Robertson Unit in Abilene. "We went back and revisited our staff, looking at our back gate procedures and the like."

Similarly, J. Keith Price, warden of the Clements Unit in Amarillo, conducted a security drill that involved the entire prison and initiated a special refresher-training course aimed at maintenance employees. According to Price, training inmates for the maintenance departments is something of a contradiction of logic and common sense. On the one hand, due to the tremendous amount of training involved, inmates who are serving lengthy sentences and aren't going anywhere are usually chosen to work in the maintenance department. On the other hand, it is these same inmates who have a greater motivation to escape.

"Nobody's got as much insider knowledge into a unit's weaknesses as maintenance crews," Price said. "We reminded these employees who these inmates are."

Meanwhile, as Texas and the nation searched for the elusive escapees, Connally Unit Correctional Officer Randy Albert, 38, began talking to the media regarding the day of the escape, relating what happened and touching on how prison officials treated him and other employees afterward. He said that he was simply in the wrong place at the wrong time that day when he stopped by the maintenance office to pick up a hitch pin to hook a gator and a trailer together so he could haul lumber.

"When I stepped up to turn into the warehouse, there were two inmates there," Albert said. "And I looked down, and saw a two-way radio and a bunch of keys laying there. At that minute I knew something was wrong, but by the time it clicked, they jumped me."

Wearing a brace on his right arm from injury caused by being handcuffed too tightly, Albert was on paid leave but expressed doubts that he would return to work.

"When I was in that room and they first blindfolded me, I figured it's going to be all right," Albert said. "They hadn't killed anybody and were saying they wouldn't . . . Inmate Rodriguez was in there, and he stuck something against my temple. I guess it was the back end of a shank or something. It was flat. He stuck it against my temple and said, 'With three pounds of pressure I'll shove this through your head. If you move I will kill you . . .' I got worried. He was talking crazy about . . . cutting ears for trophies— weird stuff like that."

Albert said that he remains haunted by that day, and takes medication in order to sleep.

"For the longest time I came home and it was hard for me to come into the house," Albert said. "I didn't know if there was somebody on the other side of the door . . . a lot of times when I lay down, as soon as I do everything starts playing over again. Once I get to sleep, my wife says I toss and turn at night."

While all indications were that the prison system was gearing up to lay the blame on the guards and other employees for the escape, Albert, as well as other employees, said the blame belonged with the administration that permitted inadequate guard training and tolerated chronic manpower shortages. The day after the escape, Albert said, he observed a notice on the wall in the personnel office indicating that the Connally Unit was 77 guards short.

"They're putting the blame on the officers, but it's just like I said, you're just out there [doing what you were trained to do]," Albert said. "The administration up there, they're supposed to run that unit. If they're saying that procedures weren't followed, that's a violation of policy . . . I don't have a problem with being corrected if I'm doing something wrong, I expect to be because if I'm doing it wrong what's gonna happen? It's going to get done wrong every time. If I'm doing wrong, why wasn't somebody there telling me so that way I can do it right?

"All I could do is listen," Albert recalled, as his coworkers struggled to free themselves. He was gagged and couldn't ask questions, and his eyes were covered with duct tape and he could not see what was taking place. "We were kind of piled up in there. The only thing they kept telling me was don't resist. If I didn't resist, they wouldn't hurt me. I didn't have a whole lot of choice. I didn't give them any reason to want to come after me.

"One of the guys got loose. Another had a knife. They started getting out . . . then I could hear the guys trying to get in because I could hear the scuffling and stuff where they were trying to hold the door shut . . . they were still there, trying to get in. I just kept thinking, don't get loud because they're going to hear us . . . I heard [a co-worker] telling them, 'Look, ya'll just go leave us be, we're not going to come out, we're not going to bother you,' because if they had gotten in there they'd probably killed all of us because I guess they weren't planning on anyone getting loose anytime soon."

One of the inmates, he said, tried to get back in. He shoved his arm through the door, but one of the victims shoved it back outside and an attempt was made to barricade the door from the inside.

"I think everybody was mad," Albert said. "We were afraid. We didn't know what they were doing. We didn't know what was happening outside . . . nobody came until the alarm went out for the escape . . . they peeled the handcuffs out of my skin. I had a quarter-inch indentation into my wrist where they had dug in. I'm not sure if I have nerve damage or not. I have tendon damage to my right wrist."

Other employees were talking privately about the day of the escape among themselves, but most would not go public for fear of reprisal from their employer.

"I'm trying to build a business of my own," Albert

said. "Yeah, I needed that paycheck. But the way they've treated me up there since it happened, I told my wife it ain't worth it . . . I've gone up there," he said, for interviews with the administration about the escape, "but it's been real hard. I see the inmates work up there around the front of the building, and I've been real nervous whenever they walk around me."

Albert told MSNBC Investigative Reports regarding the TDCJ. "All they're worried about is having a body there to hold up a uniform."

CHAPTER
7

Although the Texas 7 had been gone from the Connally Unit for nearly ten days, prison board chairman A.M. "Mac" Stringfellow publicly vowed that all seven prisoners would be apprehended. He told a concerned public the escape was not the usual spontaneous and unplanned breakout in which the fleeing prisoner is either caught in the act or shortly afterward, and admitted that this group of prisoners was cunning in their planning and execution in their break for freedom.

"They are not your typical inmate with an eighth-grade education," Stringfellow said. "They actually are pretty smart."

According to Stringfellow and other prison officials, the seven convicts were just the type of violent criminals that prompted fearful voters to pass bond measures amounting to $2.3 billion for building new prisons in the late 1980s and early 1990s. It was also the same type of violent criminal that motivated the Texas Legislature to enact much tougher sentencing laws to keep such offenders behind bars for mandatory periods of time. Later, especially following the breakout of the Texas 7, it was these tough laws that prompted many people, inmates and citizens alike, to begin believing that instead of achieving the desired results, they presented a feeling of hopelessness and despair that actually motivated prisoners to make bids for freedom. The laws certainly hadn't succeeded as a deterrent—violent crime was rampant in the State of Texas as well as across the nation—and those incarcerated under the new laws had little or no chance at rehabilitation, making their chances of assimilating back into society as free men or women next to nothing. In other words, those serving lengthy sentences of 40 or 50 years, sometimes more, easily developed the attitude that they had little to lose. What would they do to them for trying to escape? Add more time to their sentence? So what? The inevitability of additional prison time would certainly do little, if anything, to prevent the boldest of inmates from trying to break out of prison under the right conditions.

Although Texas officials would never subscribe to such a notion, nor would most law enforcement officials in most states, at least not openly, it is a fact that three of the Texas 7—Randy Halprin, Patrick Murphy, and Donald Newbury—left behind letters in the guard tower in which they talked about the "tyranny of the Texas prison system," alluding to feelings of hopelessness and despair that arise out of such tough laws and sentencing guidelines. They also wrote in the same tone about creating a revolution among the inmate population. The line that one of them quoted from the song, "Me and Bobby McGee," "Freedom's just another word for nothing left to lose," was a testament to their feelings and to current attitudes. And the fact that they had armed themselves so heavily indicated that they were on a mission of some sort—just what, nobody knew.

"They are apparently on a mission, and it's a pretty dark mission," said FBI spokeswoman Lori Bailey in an interview with the *Dallas Morning News*. "Does anybody know what that is right now? I don't think anybody does." The only thing law enforcement officials knew for certain was stated in one of the letters the inmates left behind: "You haven't heard the last of us yet." Precisely what that meant was anybody's guess at this point.

Regardless of how desperate or how hopeless these inmates were, and regardless of their mission, one thing was certain: These were very bad guys who were capable of just about anything. Even though it is possible to identify inmates who probably don't deserve the types of sentences being handed out under the new laws, unfortunate by-products of a get-tough-with-criminals society that has become fed up with being wantonly victimized, it was clear enough that those laws were intended for the likes of the Texas 7 and everyone agreed, citizens and law enforcement officials alike, that it was in the public's best interest to get them back behind bars as soon as possible.

Following the escape, some people who were close to some of the inmates were naturally fearful that one or all of the escapees might pay them a visit. It was such fear that caused Randy Halprin's adoptive parents to leave town, and prompted Joseph Garcia's parents to visit friends in another county for an extended period. Others, like Michael Rodriguez's parents, who remained at home in the same brick house in the upper-class San Antonio neighborhood where they raised their sons, chose to keep a low profile and not talk about their sons.

"It hurts too much," said their mother. "If you are a parent or a grandparent, you'd understand." Neither she, nor her husband, Raul, who still ran the convenience store near Kelly Air Force Base that he owned since his sons were youngsters, had seen or heard from Michael after the escape. Even though they had no reason to disbelieve Rodriguez's parents, the police kept their home under close surveillance for a number of days.

Many people, particularly those involved in law enforcement, began to openly speculate whether the Texas 7 were even still together or whether they had split up and had gone their separate ways. Mac Stringfellow was among those who believed that they had split up, as was Jack Dean, a retired captain in the Texas Rangers and currently a U.S. marshal in San Antonio, whose marshals were checking leads and keeping an eye on George Rivas's friends and relatives in El Paso. The truth was, nobody knew for sure whether they were still together or not, just like nobody knew where they were hiding out. The trail had gone cold following the Pearland Radio Shack robbery, with only unconfirmed scattered sightings called in by citizens from a number of locales, from San Antonio to Dallas, El Paso to Houston, and elsewhere throughout the state. None of the leads were panning out, and it seemed likely that the fugitives would remain hidden until they came out to commit another robbery.

"How much longer they will continue to be hunkered down is of great concern to law enforcement," TDCJ spokesman Glen Castlebury said. "They have avoided the kind of movement that would lead to their making a mistake that would lead to their capture."

Meanwhile, as the manhunt continued on high alert status, State Senator Carlos Truan, a Democrat from Corpus Christi, urged the Texas Legislature to investigate how the prison system had failed in allowing the Texas 7 to escape in broad daylight.

"I think the people of Texas want to know what problems developed that caused the escape of these violent criminals and what's being done to prevent further escapes," Truan said. "The legislature would also like to know in light of the fact that we've appropriated billions of dollars to the prison system and are being asked to appropriate a half-billion dollars more this legislative session. This escape doesn't speak well of the prison system."

In the meantime, all that the hundreds of law enforcement officers on the case could do was wait for the Texas 7 to make their next move.

Although the police didn't know it, they wouldn't have to wait very long.

CHAPTER

8

Using darkness as a cloak, the Texas 7 slipped out of their Econo Lodge motel room at night and began scouting around the Dallas metroplex for their next target. They needed money and clothing before they moved on, and they needed it fast. Using the police scanners that they had stolen from the Radio Shack in Pearland, they were reasonably confident that the authorities did not suspect that they were in the Dallas-Fort Worth area. It didn't take long before they settled on an Oshman's Sporting Goods store in nearby Irving for their next robbery. George Rivas had robbed an Oshman's before with one accomplice and, although he was later caught and sent to prison for that heist, he felt confident that with all the help he now had he could pull off a successful robbery there and get away before the police realized that they were the perpetrators. After discussing it with the others, they decided that December 24, Christmas Eve, would be a good day to hold up the store. Rivas was counting on a large take because of all the last minute shoppers.

As it turned out, it would become a heist worthy of a Hollywood movie.

The escaped convicts arrived at the Oshman's located at State Highway 183 and Beltline Road just before the store's six P.M. closing time. At least three of them were wearing dark pants, gray shirts, and dark hats that read SECURITY. The same three men had arm patches on their shirts that read, APS, the name of a security service. They were wandering around the store, pretending that they were doing their last-minute Christmas shopping while they posed as off-duty security guards. One store employee later recalled that they looked like the security guards that work in the schools.

Shortly after six, after the last of the legitimate customers had exited the store and the security gates had been closed, the three men approached the store managers and asked them to call all of the employees to a counter at the front of the store. They explained that they wanted to show the employees a number of photographs of young people who had been recently robbing businesses in the area. The managers, believing the request was legitimate, complied. As soon as all of the employees were gathered at the counter, one of the three men pulled out a pistol and pointed it in the air. Even then the employees didn't think that a robbery was taking place; they merely thought that they were being shown what would happen if one of the robbers that the "security agents" were telling them about showed up. In fact, the employees didn't suspect that anything was amiss until one of the workers attempted to make a telephone call to a friend.

"Hang up the phone!" one of the men commanded, waving a gun and announcing that a robbery was in progress.

The gunmen then forced the employees to place their hands on the glass counter and frisked them. Their wallets, cash, and identification were taken, as were a number of pocketknives that some of the employees had been carrying. They were then forced to form a straight line and were ordered to walk to the back of the store to the employee break room. Everyone, except for the store's manager, Wesley Farris, was forced to face a wall and kneel down. In an apparent show of force designed as a warning to the others to cooperate, one employee was roughed up by one of the robbers, who punched him in the ribs and slammed his head against the wall.

"If you don't fuck up, you'll see Christmas," one of the thieves said to the employees.

Similar to the methods used in the breakout of the Connally Unit, some of the employees were bound with plastic zip-ties and others were tied up with their belts. Each employee was forced to cross his or her legs, which the thieves then bound with rope.

At one point one of the robbers, presumably the leader, told the others, "If you kill one of them, you'll have to kill them all."

Satisfied that the employees were securely bound and would not cause them any problems, the thieves took Farris, the store manager, and forced him to open the store's safe. Three cash deposits totaling more than $70,000 for Christmas Eve's receipts had been placed in the safe, and they took all of it. They also went through each of the store's cash registers and removed cash and checks. Afterward, still forcing Farris to accompany them, they went around the store and took at least 40 guns, and plenty of ammunition. Then they filled a couple of shopping carts full of winter clothing and other supplies. By 6:25 P.M. they were ready to exit by the store's rear freight door. Before leaving, they took the keys to Farris's Ford Explorer, forcing him to tell them where it was parked.

They might have gotten away unscathed had it not been for an off-duty employee who, from outside the store, noticed their suspicious activity through a window and called the police.

Officer Aubrey Hawkins, a 29-year-old rookie cop who had been with the Irving Police Department for only 14 months, was down the street a few hundred yards at an Olive Garden restaurant enjoying a Christmas Eve dinner with his wife and nine-year-old son when the call came in about the suspicious activity at Oshman's. Hawkins announced to his wife and son that he had to take the call, and he dutifully left the restaurant and took off for the sporting goods store in his police cruiser. None of them realized that it would be the last time he would see his family.

Hawkins arrived at the same time that another officer arrived, about three minutes after the call. Hawkins went to the rear of the store, and the other officer went to the store's front; additional officers were en route. George Rivas and some of the others were exiting the freight door as Hawkins pulled up. The gunfire that followed occurred quickly. Farris, hearing the gunfire and unaware that officers were already on the scene, called the police and began untying the employees.

The barrage of gunfire could easily be heard by the employees inside the store as well as by anyone passing by. Hawkins was shot, literally assassinated in a hail of gunfire, through the windows of his cruiser. According to what store employees would later tell the police, at least 20 to 25 shots had been fired, in rapid succession. Hawkins hadn't stood a chance against the surprise attack and hadn't even been afforded the opportunity to try and speed away to save his life.

It all had happened so quickly. After disabling Hawkins by shooting him through his car windows, the assailants dragged him out of his car and shot him several more times, in the head and the back. His attackers stole his handgun and, after climbing into their getaway car, Farris's Ford Explorer, ran over Hawkins's head three times.

The next officer to arrive found Hawkins lying on the parking lot near his car, mortally wounded. The officer called for medical assistance as a SWAT team raced toward the store, but it was too late for the fallen officer. Hawkins died at Parkland Memorial Hospital in Dallas shortly after his arrival.

When the SWAT team arrived, they immediately surrounded the building, not knowing whether any of the suspects were still inside. When it was determined that all of the suspects had fled the scene, the SWAT team entered the store and brought out all of the employees. The employees were transported to the Irving Police Department, where each of them provided a statement regarding what had occurred. They also were shown photographs of possible suspects, including photos of the Texas 7, to see if they could identify any of the thieves. Several of the Texas 7 inmates were identified, but the police would not publicly announce which ones. The store employees ended up spending most of the night talking to the investigators, but were allowed to go home early Christmas morning. Although the police had earlier been led to believe that only three suspects had been involved in the robbery and subsequent murder of Officer Hawkins, after interviewing the store employees all night they felt that all seven of the escapees were involved.

Meanwhile, the investigators spent most of the night collecting evidence at the Oshman's store, and, with the help of the store's managers, they conducted an inventory of the store's merchandise to determine exactly what was taken during the robbery.

"Their intentions were unclear whether they were going for money or merchandise," said Irving Police Department spokesman David Tull.

Although the police were releasing few details about the robbery and shooting initially, Tull did tell reporters that Farris's Ford Explorer was used as the getaway vehicle and had been found about a half mile from the store. The fact that they ditched the vehicle so close to the store was an indication that they either had another car waiting nearby, or someone, possibly one or more of the Texas 7 themselves, had followed those in the getaway car from the store to the location where it was abandoned.

There was also another possibility: They had outside help.

There were many things that bothered the police about this case, especially after the police felt sure that the Oshman's store had been held up by the Texas 7 and one of their own had been killed in the process. How had the escapees managed to obtain the hats and the gray shirts with the name of a security company patched onto them? Escapees who were in such high profile throughout the state as the Texas 7 likely wouldn't take the chance of coming out of hiding to try and find such items on their own. It would be too risky. It seemed more likely, and made more sense, that someone outside of their group had assisted them in finding those items—but the police had no idea who.

Another thing that bothered the investigators was how these thugs had so mercilessly gunned down Aubrey Hawkins before he had a chance to even get out of his car, and then cold-bloodedly ran over his head and body three times before fleeing. The robbery and murder were a clear indication of how far they would go to remain free. But the fact that they had now murdered a cop would push authorities to go that much further to catch them.

Nobody kills a cop and gets away with it for long. Nobody.

CHAPTER
9

In the aftermath of policeman Aubrey Hawkins's slaying, local, state, and federal agencies significantly stepped up their efforts to find the elusive Texas 7. The public was outraged and frightened over such savagery unleashed on one of their keepers of the peace, and the law enforcement community wanted vengeance. In addition to carrying their usual side arms, patrol units began carrying additional weapons, such as extra shotguns inside their cars just in case they encountered the escapees. It was rumored that some officers in Dallas were also carrying Israeli-made submachine guns. With a reputation for fierce retribution against criminals that dated back to the days of Bonnie and Clyde and before, everyone in

Texas's law enforcement circles wanted to make sure that what happened to Hawkins would not be easily repeated. If such a violent encounter occurred again, they wanted to make sure they were equipped to get the convicts first.

The local police and the federal agencies had no idea where the escapees might have gone following Hawkins's murder. They had received reports that they had been seen in central Texas, in Oklahoma, and Louisiana, and as far away as Colorado, but none of the leads panned out. Furthermore, no one discounted the possibility that the seven convicts had fled to Mexico even though security along the borders was still tight, but there was nothing to indicate that they had headed south of the border, either.

"We've got every agency you can think of working on this," said Larry Todd, a spokesman for the Texas prison system. "Federal marshals, FBI, Texas Rangers, police, sheriffs' departments. We've had a lot of leads that weren't successful, but we're chasing down every one . . . these people are very cunning, very street smart. We have to exercise a lot of patience."

In nearby Dalworthington Gardens, where Randy Halprin was from, police officers were being especially cautious after the shooting death of officer Hawkins, according to Chief Bill Waybourn.

"We are on heightened alert and have extra folks out there keeping very much a vigil watch," Waybourn said. "These are very desperate people. Officers need to be very vigilant. These guys are not going to hesitate. That's why we have to be prepared to act immediately."

Despite the airing of a reenactment of the prison escape on the December 16 episode of *America's Most Wanted,* eight days before the Oshman's robbery, there were no new viable leads on their whereabouts, even though the show had prompted several phone calls from people who thought that they had seen the fugitives. Plans were being made to air additional segments about the Texas 7 on future episodes, including details of the Oshman's robbery and Hawkins's slaying. Unless the fugitives were apprehended first.

Although a number of people had expressed that they believed that the Texas 7 had split up, this line of thinking had, of course, been dismissed following the holdup of the Oshman's sporting goods store and the death of Officer Hawkins. Although it appeared doubtful that the seven inmates were still anywhere near Dallas, the police throughout that area remained on highest alert. Police officers on horseback searched wooded areas, and more than the usual number of helicopters flew around the city's skyline looking for suspicious activity on the ground. Police also handed out wanted posters and flyers, with photos and descriptions of the escapees, at many of the city's shopping malls, and before long Domino's Pizza began plastering photos of the Texas 7 on their pizza boxes. Despite all of the efforts being made, however, the police were not one step closer to locating and apprehending the Texas 7, and with each passing hour that they remained free, the greater the embarrassment became for the Texas Department of Criminal Justice.

As additional details of the escape began to filter out from within the prison system, more questions arose to suggest that perhaps the inmates might have had help from one or more members of the prison staff. An expert in criminal justice, Professor Larry Sullivan, of New York City's John Jay College, voiced his opinion that it was "highly unusual" to leave dangerous inmates unsupervised for any period of time, and even more unusual for weapons to be attained so easily by inmates. Nonetheless, there was no evidence, at least not at this point, to indicate that the prisoners had any kind of inside assistance.

One of the problems that may have contributed to the Connally Unit breakout, according to Gary Johnson, prison director for the TDCJ, is the seriously outdated method used for classifying inmates as security risks. Since the present system was implemented in 1984, the state's inmate population has more than tripled. That same inmate population has also become more dangerous, due in part to laws that were enacted lengthening sentences for a number of crimes. It was revealed that two of the Texas 7 inmates had previously made attempts to escape, but because of their recent behavior they had been reclassified as trustees.

If things weren't hot enough already for the Texas prison system, the state Senate's Criminal Justice Committee turned up the heat even more following the slaying of Officer Hawkins, announcing that they would be holding a hearing on the Connally Unit escape in the near future. Among the things that were on the agenda for discussion was the new prisoner classification system, which, according to Gary Johnson, should be in place by March 1, 2001.

Several state senators appeared dismayed by the emerging details of the escape, particularly because those details were showing that several opportunities to foil the breakout had been missed. The senators indicated that they had difficulty understanding how a prison employee could notice that three prisoners were unsupervised and not report it, and why a correctional officer in the central control unit failed to report the fire alarm that had been tripped by the guards when they were were locked inside the electrical room.

"So many people seem like they don't want to know what is happening," Senator Steve Ogden said. "It seems to me like a systemic problem."

"This is a tragic, one-time, isolated event," countered Mac Stringfellow. "What happened down in Connally is certainly not systemic . . . it's a tough situation, I'm not denying that. I think we're doing the best we can with what we've got."

What they had, it was pointed out, was a strained prison system, holding approximately 160,000 inmates in 116 prisons, near its capacity. They also had a dramatic increase in incidents of violence committed by inmates against correctional officers. At the Connally Unit alone, according to the *Fort Worth Star-Telegram*, there were 752 reported assaults against employees since the prison opened in 1995, more than at any other Texas prison unit. Due to the dangerous conditions and low pay, prison correctional officers were leaving the system in large numbers; one out of every five guards resigned in 1999 and 2000. The numbers translated into a shortage of about 2,500 guards system wide.

Meanwhile, it was revealed that blood from three different people, including Officer Hawkins, was found inside the abandoned Ford Explorer that had been used as the getaway car in the Oshman's robbery. It was believed that Hawkins's blood was transferred to the getaway car by one of the escapees who pulled the wounded and bleeding officer out of his own car. The investigators were not saying much about the evidence, however: part of the strategy being implemented by the FBI and the other agencies involved stopping the flow of information to the press. As such, it was not known whether any of the escaped convicts had been shot or had sustained some other type of wound that would have caused them to sustain blood loss. Because the escapees had taken Hawkins's gun with them when they fled, investigators were unable to determine whether Hawkins had returned fire at his assailants. However, according to Jayne Hawkins, the slain officer's mother, the police had indicated to her that one or more of the Texas 7 might have been seriously injured by their own crossfire during their ambush. Mrs. Hawkins indicated that, because of different trajectories of 11 bullets that hit her son, more than one of the inmates had fired at him.

According to the autopsy report, Officer Hawkins was shot six times in the head, once in the back, and four times in his left arm. The bulletproof vest he was wearing protected his chest from two other shots. Despite repeated attempts to talk with the police about Hawkins's slaying, additional information about his death and the Oshman's robbery was not made available to the family or to the public.

"If there is something that would help, I would hope they would figure it out and release it," said Curtis Hawkins, officer Hawkins's father. "Knowing that would help the search. If you go out there, you can see where the bullets might have ricocheted. I can see how they might have hurt each other."

Due to the lack of viable leads in the case, an argument was being made by not only the news media but by others as well, such as Dr. Richard Ward, a former New York City police detective and the dean of the College of Criminal Justice at Sam Houston State University in Huntsville, that certain information should be released to help further the investigation along.

"After a period of time, it would make sense to put it out there," Dr. Ward said. Keeping the information private, he continued, could prove detrimental to locating and capturing the escapees. He cited the Unabomber case as an example in which the sharing of information ended up helping the police.

"The glaring example of this is the Ted Kaczynski case," Dr. Ward said. "They kept a lot of information from the public and then they released the manifesto and his brother recognized him. That's the classic case of why it's better to release information."

The information was apparently also being withheld from officers involved peripherally in the investigation, who complained that they had been unable to obtain details regarding the Oshman's crime scene. They argued that it might be helpful to publicize information such as the amount of blood found at the crime scene and whether the amount was typical of a gunshot wound or some other type of wound, such as a cut from a broken piece of glass. Healthcare workers, for example, if alerted to how much blood the escapees might have lost, could better look out for a wounded person seeking treatment.

"There are going to be certain things that only certain people will know," countered Irving police officer David Tull. "Is it crucial? We don't know. It could turn out to be a turning point . . . we don't know what type of injuries they have. Anything is possible. Did they cut themselves on glass? Did they mash their hands? Did they get shot? We just don't know. We don't know if Officer Hawkins returned fire, because we don't have his weapon."

The reason for the clampdown on the release of information, according to Glen Castlebury was a general fear among law enforcement personnel that the escapees might be learning too much from news reports about what the authorities were doing to find them. FBI and the Irving Police Department also asserted that reporters had revealed information that could have placed police officers in danger. Even though Castlebury would not elaborate, he said that there was one instance in which it was believed that reporters might have inadvertently foiled an opportunity to capture the escapees.

Rob Wiley, the president of the Freedom of Information Foundation of Texas, strongly disagreed and argued that withholding such information could lead to public mistrust about how the authorities were handling the search for the Texas 7.

"I would be very skeptical of the idea that the media is the reason they haven't caught these guys," Wiley said. "The public wants to know what's up with these guys, and they want to be reassured of their safety. When you make that kind of statement, you ought to have something to back it up . . . there's a line between whatever legitimate reasons for withholding information and causing mistrust from the public."

Meanwhile, only days after officer Hawkins was killed, federal weapons charges were filed against the Texas 7 by the U.S. Bureau of Alcohol, Tobacco, and Firearms, widening the federal role in the hunt for the escapees. Broadening the government's role even more, the FBI indicated that it was preparing to file separate charges against the seven for unlawful flight to avoid prosecution. All of these charges were in addition to the murder charges filed against them for killing Hawkins. Federal officials believed that the inmates were still together as a group.

As officer Aubrey Hawkins was being laid to rest, it was announced that a $100,000 reward had been offered for information leading to the arrest and indictment of the Texas 7. The reward was made possible by a community effort of citizens and businesses in and around Irving, the Irving Police Department, and the federal government. The reward was made in light of the fact that authorities now believed more than ever that the Texas 7 were receiving aid such as food, shelter, and other types of assistance by a person or persons outside their group. It was hoped that the reward would motivate someone with information, perhaps even the person or persons providing the assistance or someone close to them, to come forward. However, there were no immediate takers, and according to TDCJ spokesman Larry Todd, the situation remained "status quo." No one had a clue to the fugitives' whereabouts, and it seemed like the chances of a peaceful resolution to the situation had become even further removed.

"While we're prayerful and hopeful, we're not optimistic," Todd said. "This is an extremely dangerous scenario of which we can't downplay any aspect . . . the outside help they are receiving is giving them a big advantage, but with patience and diligence, we think some law enforcement agency will locate the escapees."

CHAPTER

10

On Tuesday, December 26, 2000, just two days after the Oshman's robbery and the murder of officer Aubrey Hawkins, police in Arlington, a suburb southwest of Dallas, received a tip from an employee at the Amerisuites Hotel near Six Flags Over Texas, located at the Road to Six Flags and Highway 360. According to the tip, a group of women told hotel employees that they believed the men they had been with at the hotel the night before and early that morning might have been some of the escaped convicts.

The police acted quickly on the tip and surrounded the Amerisuites Hotel with SWAT teams. They quietly and quickly evacuated three floors of the hotel and a nearby auto dealership, and focused their attention on the room in which they believed their suspects were. The men, it turned out, came out peacefully and the episode proved to be yet another embarrassment for the Texas authorities. After talking to the men and comparing them to photos of the Texas 7, it was quickly decided that a case of mistaken identity had been made. The men in the hotel room were from El Paso, and they were in Arlington on business.

"It turned out to be some bad information," said Sergeant James Hawthorne of the Arlington Police Department. "The people that they thought were these suspects were not the suspects, so the search continues."

In the days following the murder, particularly just prior to and right after Hawkins's burial, the mood of the community and of the police force became more evident. Residents, friends, relatives, and his colleagues on the police force turned the entrance to Oshman's sporting goods store into a shrine of sorts, placing flowers there. The store was closed temporarily in honor of the fallen officer, and a prayer vigil was held there one evening. The grief displayed at the prayer vigil was overwhelming at times, and it generated a mood of pessimism regarding the apprehension of the murdering fugitives.

"He was a good, solid kid, and we're going to miss him," said Tim Kelly, Hawkins's night shift commander. "He was absolutely excited about his job."

"It's very somber around here," said Irving police

spokesman David Tull. "We've got the tough guy image, but even these guys need to break down . . . I haven't heard anything but good things about the man. His supervisor was telling me about what a good person and a good police officer he was." Tull wore a strip of black tape over his badge that carried a message written in Latin, NO ONE ASSAILS ME WITH IMPUNITY.

According to those closest to him, Hawkins was dedicated to fighting crime and had made it his goal to make a difference. He was known as a kind man who had held a dream to make the world a better place by fighting crime. It was unfortunate that his young life was cut short before he could make his life's goals a reality.

The memorial service for Aubrey Hawkins was held less than a mile from the Oshman's Sporting Goods store where he was slain. Several in attendance recalled him as a good-natured man who lived for his family and died performing the duties of the job he loved. Being a police officer, one mourner stated, had been his lifelong ambition. One of Hawkins's lifelong friends told mourners how he had grown up with Aubrey and had watched him grow from a "tall, lanky, goofy kid" into a man, a dedicated police officer, a husband and father.

In order to allow Hawkins's colleagues to attend his funeral service, the Irving Police Department asked dozens on non-uniformed officers to put on uniforms to take the places of those who chose to pay their final respects. Aside from the officers from Irving, there were more than 2,000 police from across Texas who attended to pay their respects. In a touching moment, Hawkins's mother, Jayne, made an impassioned plea for police officers and the public alike to forgive those who had killed her son.

"Those people who did that to Aubrey, don't hate them," she said.

"He didn't become a policeman to be a hero," said the pastor, Laurel Hallman, a longtime family friend. "He became a policeman to protect people and to uphold the law."

At one point Jayne Hawkins handed Pastor Hallman a prepared statement, which he read for her. "As a baby, he was happy and loving," the pastor read. "As a little boy, he brought dogs home to take care of. As a security officer, he took young people in trouble to their parents. My son is not gone. He is in my heart, alive and sweet, kind, loving, helpful and strong."

"It's not how Aubrey died that made him my hero—it's how he lived," said Irving Police Chief Lowell Cannaday at the memorial service.

In the meantime, the League of United Latin-American Citizens Council Number 1, a civil rights organization located in Corpus Christi, publicly announced that they wanted to make certain that the Texas Legislature held oversight hearings to establish accountability as to how and why the Texas 7 had been able to accomplish their breakout so easily.

"What is lacking at these facilities?" asked Mary Helen Salazar, the group's president. "We just can't understand how and why these convicts were able to escape."

The group was assured that oversight hearings would indeed occur, and that an official report outlining an internal investigation of the prison breakout would be forthcoming.

As the massive manhunt continued to sweep across Texas and into bordering states, the investigators chased dozens of tips that got them nowhere.

Then, on December 31, a fireworks stand was robbed in Dallas, a week to the day after Hawkins's slaying. Brandishing firearms, three men wearing bandanas and camouflage clothing broke into the fireworks stand and surprised sleeping employees, whom they quickly bound with duct tape. One of the thieves purportedly stated, "We're not going back to prison." After taking $3,400 in cash, a .38-caliber pistol, and fireworks, the three men fled in a Dodge Dakota pickup that was owned by one of the employees.

Although the TDCJ quickly came out and said that they didn't believe the fireworks stand robbery was committed by the Texas 7, the Dallas County Sheriff's Department said that they weren't too sure and had not ruled out such a possibility.

"I don't have any evidence that they did or didn't do the robbery," said Investigator Don Peritz, Jr.

"We're waiting to hear back on the physical evidence collected from the scene . . . everybody's so paranoid. The tension is really, really thick. We're not resting until these guys are caught. Any call could be the call."

Despite everyone's best efforts, the multifaceted investigation was going nowhere, at least it wasn't going anywhere anytime soon. About the only thing that the police seemed to agree on was that they did not believe that the Texas 7 would give up easily.

"Do they have something else planned?" asked Tull. "I wish I had a crystal ball. I think we should expect the worst."

"We're very surprised to see that these convicts are still all together," said Lori Bailey, a spokeswoman for the Dallas office of the FBI. "That's highly unusual, in that it doesn't lend itself to concealment. That's just an indicator of how bold they are, how brash they are, and of how dangerous they are . . . the charges enhance the investigation. It makes it a more regional and national search."

"I think the act that we believe they've committed certainly underscores what we've said from the outset," said Larry Fitzgerald, a spokesman for the TDCJ, who added that it was unusual that the seven convicts had remained together after their escape. "These are desperate and dangerous people."

"Our biggest fear is that someone will get hurt because of the firepower they have," said TDCJ spokesman Larry Todd. "We are approaching this as though they have a plan of some sort. What that is, who knows?"

According to ATF agent Tom Crowley, the weaponry and ammunition stolen from Oshman's was more than enough to cause a lot of damage and take a lot of lives.

"It was a diverse amount of weapons and different types," said Crowley. "In conjunction with the Irving Police Department, we don't want to go into specifics right now. But there were different types of weapons and different caliber of weapons . . . there is an awful lot of weapons at their disposal, and it does concern us a great deal. Out of the Oshman's store, there were 40 weapons stolen."

The New Year brought additional suspected sightings of the Texas 7. On Thursday, January 4, 2001, witnesses reported that they had seen at least two of the escapees, George Rivas and Michael Rodriguez, in the parking lot of a Bank of America in San Marcos, a medium-sized town a few miles northeast of San Antonio.

The police were actually called to the bank at approximately 12:45 P.M. by one of the bank's clerks who wanted to report a man who asked to open an account but was acting "odd." After getting bad vibes from the man and sensing that something was not right, the clerk called the police.

"The man made the employees nervous," the bank clerk told the police.

A witness who had been outside the bank told the

police that he had seen seven or eight men standing around three vehicles in the parking lot. The man who was acting "odd" inside the bank joined those outside in the parking lot after coming out of the building. Prior to the arrival of the police, they got inside their cars and headed out of town toward the Interstate 35 on-ramp.

When shown photographs of the Texas 7, at least two of the witnesses confirmed that Rivas and Rodriguez had been among the men they had seen.

"We have no concrete evidence that says that the escapees were there," said Larry Todd. "We don't know where they are. That's the candid answer and it is our fervent desire that we will get them back without bloodshed."

The Texas 7 had gone north after their escape, then east, west, and now south, all within the borders of Texas. While it was possible that they were finally heading for Mexico, now that they had gone south to San Marcos, no one could be sure because they had not appeared to be in any kind of a hurry to leave the state.

"I don't have any idea what these guys are doing," said San Marcos Police Commander Bill Glasgow. "None of us really do. It's pretty clear it doesn't look like they are leaving the state. I don't have any explanation why they are going the way they are ... we're very concerned about the safety of our officers," he said, adding that most of the authorities expect some kind of a "violent confrontation" with the escapees at some point.

As the sightings of the Texas 7 continued, the Police Department in Denton, Texas, a community just north of Dallas, received more than 100 reported sightings that same day, January 4. Callers reported seeing the escaped convicts all over town, at stores like Kmart, Wal-Mart, a 7-Eleven convenience store, a Conoco gas station, even a Denny's restaurant. However, authorities quickly discounted the calls when none of them panned out, blaming them on local talk radio stations.

"Somehow somebody told somebody, and it made it all the way to talk radio," said policeman Scott Salazar. "We got a lot of talk radio. They were rumors, purely rumors."

Even later that day the escapees were reported as having been seen as far north as Colorado. Colorado police warned residents in the southwest part of the state that the convicts might be passing through. Before long the police in Canon City, Colorado, located just southwest of Colorado Springs, received an anonymous report that the seven convicts had been seen driving a red Ford panel van. The caller had provided the police with a license number, 48366, but not the corresponding state that it was from, and the number could not be traced. The report was written up as unconfirmed.

As far as the authorities in Texas were concerned, the escapees were still moving about their state, possibly in the Dallas-Fort Worth area, driving two late-model, four-door compact cars, one of which was believed to be a Toyota Camry and the other a Honda Accord. One of the vehicles was listed as black and the other silver, but the authorities didn't know which vehicle was which color.

The truth of the matter was that the convicts could have been anywhere after leaving the San Marcos area, some 210 miles south of Dallas, and no one really had a clue as to their whereabouts.

CHAPTER

11

The breakout of the Texas 7 was not only an embarrassment to the Texas prison system, it was a source of bafflement to the criminologists following the case and to those who were assisting in the search for the convicts. According to retired FBI criminal-behavior expert Gregg McCrary, who spoke to *Newsweek* magazine and MSNBC nearly a month after the prison break, jailbreaks involving multiple prisoners are rare and it is nearly unheard of for a band of "probably psychopaths with no loyalty to a group" to remain together for such an extended period of time.

"This group is very, very dangerous," McCrary told *Newsweek*. "Now that they have killed a policeman, there isn't much left for them to lose."

One of the Oshman's employees also spoke to *Newsweek* about the same time that McCrary did, describing George Rivas as the person giving out the orders to the other robbers.

"I got the impression he didn't want to hurt anybody, but he would if it was necessary," the employee, who did not wish to be identified, told *Newsweek*. "A couple of the other ones, they gave me the idea they would hurt us in a heartbeat."

The employee explained that the carefully planned robbery began when Rivas came in just before closing time and identified himself as an official of a local security company. He asked for one of the managers by name, which he could only have known if he had come into the store previously to case it, or if he had made telephone calls to the store. By that time other members of the group had already entered the store and were pretending to be shopping. After talking to the manager and arranging for all of the store's employees to gather around the front counter, Rivas made his move and began pointing the gun he was carrying toward the ceiling.

"When I turned around, Rivas was standing with a .357 Magnum pointed at my chest," said the employee. "He said, 'Don't do anything, because if you do I'll have to shoot you, and if I shoot you I'll have to shoot everybody!'" which were nearly the same words that were relayed to the others via the walkie-talkies.

According to the employee, Rivas's plan had been

The rear gate of the John Connally Prison Unit, where members of the Texas 7 were mistaken by prison guards to be maintenance workers.
AP PHOTO/WIDE WORLD PHOTOS

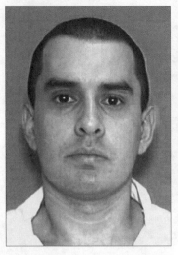
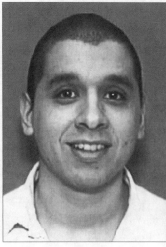

The Texas 7.
This Page Clockwise from top left: George Rivas, Joseph Garcia, Donald Newbury.

Facing Page Clockwise from top left: Larry Harper, Randy Halprin, Michael Rodriguez, Patrick Murphy, Jr.

AP PHOTO/WIDE WORLD PHOTOS

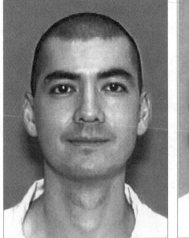

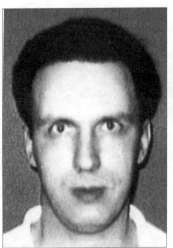

The fugitives after their arrest. *Above:* Left to right are Michael Rodriguez, George Rivas, Joseph Garcia. *Left:* Randy Halprin.
AP PHOTO/WIDE WORLD PHOTOS

Right: Patrick Murphy appears in the El Paso County jail in Colorado on January 24. Notice the drastic differences in the appearance of the fugitives compared to the mug shots that saturated the media during the manhunt.
AP PHOTO/WIDE WORLD PHOTOS

The scene at Oshman's Sporting Goods store on December 24, 2000.
AP PHOTO/WIDE WORLD PHOTOS

The mug shot of Raul Rodriguez following his arrest on February 2. Rodriguez, father of fugitive Michael Rodriguez, was charged with supplying the Texas 7 with their car following the prison break.
AP PHOTO/WIDE WORLD PHOTOS

Irving, Texas Police Officer Aubrey Hawkins. AP PHOTO/WIDE WORLD PHOTOS

Texas police officers help bury Aubrey Hawkins. AP PHOTO/WIDE WORLD PHOTOS

Gary Johnson, director of the Institutional Division of the Texas Department of Criminal Justice, answers questions using a photo of the guardroom through which the Texas 7 escaped. AP PHOTO/WIDE WORLD PHOTOS

Mac Stringfellow. AP PHOTO/WIDE WORLD PHOTOS

The Coachlight Motel and RV Park outside Woodland Park on the morning of January 22. AP PHOTO/WIDE WORLD PHOTOS

Authorities haul away the RV used by the Texas 7 during their time at the Coachlight. Around 12:40 p.m. on January 22, Larry Harper killed himself inside the vehicle. AP PHOTO/WIDE WORLD PHOTOS

The arsenal found inside the RV used by the Texas 7 is put on display during a news conference on January 25, 2001. AP PHOTO/WIDE WORLD PHOTOS

Alleged Texas 7 mastermind George Rivas appears at the Teller County Courthouse on January 25 with his lawyer, Deborah Grohs. AP PHOTO/WIDE WORLD PHOTOS

almost flawlessly executed. Rivas had correctly thought that wearing the employees' red shirts would allow the seven to move around the front part of the store after closing time without drawing attention to themselves. His biggest mistake was in not changing from the black pants they were wearing to the store employees' khaki pants. What Rivas hadn't counted on was an employee who came to the door to meet her boyfriend. She had noticed the difference in pants and considered it suspicious; that prompted her to call the police instead of attempting to gain entry.

As information about the Oshman's holdup continued to trickle out from police sources, it was finally revealed that the reason the police knew so quickly, aside from identification made by employees, that the Texas 7 had robbed the store was because they had inadvertently left behind one of the firearms that they had stolen from the prison at the time of their escape. Although detectives had been reasonably sure of who was responsible for the robbery from the outset based on the employees' statements, finding the weapon was kind of like the icing on the cake.

As the investigation continued with little or no progress, the reward money for information leading to the apprehension and indictment of the Texas 7 was suddenly doubled when an online bail bond company added $100,000 to the reward fund. It now stood at $200,000 as investigators continued to hope that it would motivate anyone harboring or helping the fu-

GARY C. KING

gitives, or anyone knowing who was helping them, to come forward, make a deal, and collect the money.

"Ultimately, I think the reward needs to be bumped up to attract some interest," said Irving Mayor Joe Putnam, as talks continued about raising the reward even more. However, much to everyone's dismay, there were no immediate takers.

Hopes were raised on Tuesday, January 9, 2001, that the police were finally making some headway toward locating the elusive fugitives when officers in Forth Worth simultaneously searched several homes that they thought might be connected to the fugitives, either through friends or relatives. Two men with outstanding warrants were arrested as a result of the search operation, but it turned out that they had no connection to the case and the police efforts ended up being fruitless.

In the meantime, after reports were broadcast indicating that five of the seven inmates were seen eating at a fast-food restaurant in Dallas, Patrick Murphy's younger half sister, Kristina Rogers, went on television and made a plea for Murphy to surrender.

"Patrick, wherever you are, just please stop this violence and turn yourself in," Kristina tearfully pleaded. "You know you weren't raised to do this. Just stop the pain that the family is going through."

At about the same time that Rogers made her tearful plea authorities formally charged Rivas and Newbury with the robbery of the Radio Shack in Pearland.

All seven inmates had previously been charged with capital murder in the death of officer Aubrey Hawkins, and prosecutors for the first time indicated that they would seek the death penalty against the fugitives if they were ever apprehended.

"If they would split up, our chances of getting them would increase," said Larry Todd, TDCJ spokesman. "Right now, they're sharing information, encouraging each other and not doing the normal things escapees do . . . we think they committed to stay together long before this escape. It's almost like a blood brother pact of swearing to keep together."

Authorities also believed that Rivas was largely responsible for holding the group together.

According to Tory Caeti, a professor at the University of North Texas, Rivas was the bonding mechanism that was holding the group together. It was Rivas's smooth-talking abilities that were helping the fugitives evade identification and capture in the largest manhunt in Texas history, Caeti told *Good Morning America*.

"It reminds me of Dillinger, or 'Baby Face' Nelson, and the gangs that used to roam from city to city robbing as they went along," Professor Caeti said as a fascinated nation watched.

"It's important to point out that these guys are in the one percent of the prison population," Caeti said. "They're using their intelligence. They've been smart enough to lay low, except during the instances they've committed robberies since their escape . . . The key is that their escape was obviously well planned. To have been out this long, they must be getting some outside help. They've made a pact to stay together, and, given the weapons they've stolen, they've made a plan not to go back to prison . . . It's highly unlikely you will find all these guys eating together somewhere at a McDonald's. If the intelligence reports are correct, these guys have broken off into smaller groups at times. They would look conspicuous if they traveled together, and they know it.

"Most of the time, when convicts are captured," Caeti continued, "it's through the help of well-meaning citizens or someone who's really in the know of their activities. Police never want to deter people from phoning in tips. But that means they have to weed through the ones sent by psychics, pranksters, and others before they come across a real fruitful lead."

According to Professor Caeti, it was not likely that the prison photos and the sketches of the fugitives would be very helpful in bringing about their apprehension. Caeti pointed out that prison photos often tend to be dated, taken when the convicts first arrive at prison and have just had their hair cut short, and their appearances are often quite different by the time the brazen ones might attempt an escape. It was also likely, said Caeti, that they would have changed their appearance by growing facial hair, dying their hair, and wearing their hair differently than they had in prison.

Meanwhile, police officers throughout the state remained on edge, especially when responding to calls involving suspected robberies at just about any kinds of stores. One such incident occurred at a Best Buy electronics store in Plano, Texas, in early January. When the Plano officers responded, they formed a perimeter around the building and evacuated the store one customer at a time.

"They said they knew exactly what they were looking for," said one of the store's customers, "and the scariest part was when they came in because they all had shotguns and their other guns drawn. They were not kidding around."

"Officers are very aware of their safety right now," said Plano Police Department Sergeant Mark Hunt. "They're taking every precaution necessary as far as themselves and as far as their partners and as far as the citizens involved . . ."

The Plano incident turned out to be a false alarm. There was no sign of the Texas 7, and the report of the robbery in progress had been a waste of everyone's time and a drain on everyone's nerves.

People, especially those in Texas, were as fearful as they were fascinated by all of the information they were getting concerning the activities of the Texas 7. People had become frightened when the lights went out due to an ice storm, almost immediately thinking that the escapees had cut the power off to their homes. Others began buying up handguns and enrolling in classes to teach them how to use them. Still others were buying security systems for their homes.

"Some people won't let their wives walk at night," said an instructor who teaches classes in the use of concealed handguns. "And every time they go into an Oshman's or a 7-Eleven, they think about it."

According to psychologists, for victims of crime, there exists a strong feeling that just about anything can happen to anyone, anywhere, at anytime.

"It's that sense that the world is simply not a safe place, that some kind of danger is everywhere," said Mary Lynn Crow, a Fort Worth psychologist. "It makes us all a little jumpy, perhaps hypervigilant."

In the meantime, Larry Todd appeared on national television and explained how the authorities in Texas had received thousands of tips regarding the fugitives' whereabouts, but none of them had proven to be useful.

"Very frankly, our leads are very, very limited," Todd told ABC News. "What we need are good solid leads. We need license plate numbers and better descriptions." Most of all, Todd said, the authorities just wanted the situation to end without any more violence.

"Our worst fear is that this will end in bloodshed . . . that's what we do not want to happen," Todd said. "But we will get these men back."

CHAPTER

12

A few days before an official report outlining the controversial and embarrassing prison breakout was due to be released to the public by the TDCJ, a memo that detailed the contents of the report was leaked to news media by someone within the prison system. The memo, which appeared in *The Dallas Morning News* and was discussed on an affiliated television news station, outlined the so-called "meticulous plan" that the seven inmates had concocted, showing in detail how they had pulled off the escape by seizing control of the prison gates and a weapons storage room. Members of the TDCJ were outraged over the leak, but no one denied the authenticity of the memo.

"The editorial content of *The Dallas Morning News*

story causes me less heartburn than how an internal memo detailing a sensitive investigation fell into the hands of the media," said Glen Castlebury.

The internal memo discussed how four of the escapees drove a truck to the prison's back gate where they overpowered an officer. It explained how one of the escapees, wearing street clothes taken from another prison employee, told the officer in the guard tower that he was there to install video surveillance equipment. The memo even quoted portions of the report: "The unsuspecting officer then allowed the disguised inmate outside the prison's perimeter fence and into the armory. Soon after ... the inmate overpowered the officer, taking control of the armory and the perimeter gates."

Upon concluding their escape plans, the memo stated that all seven inmates "then drove away from the Connally Unit undetected."

Having their dirty laundry splashed across newspapers and flashed on television screens before they were ready to face the public was hard for the prison system. Castlebury lashed back at the media by saying that reporters had misconstrued portions of the memo, and that the so-called inmate "picnic" during the lunch hour was not accurately depicted in the news media. Responding to reports indicating that the inmates had been left alone, Castlebury pointed out that a maintenance supervisor had in fact remained with the inmates while the others went to lunch.

"It wasn't like everybody walked out and said,

'Okay, inmates, take over,' " Castlebury said. "The memo was written and designed to stay in the hands of people involved in the hunt for the fugitives. I have no idea how it went from one set of hands to the other."

Other parts of the memo indicated that the official report would be laying blame for the escape on the employees and correctional officers on duty that day.

After hearing the news of the memo, Aubrey Hawkins's mother, Jayne, lashed out at the prison system and blamed the breakout on lax security and staff shortages. She said that it was negligence on the prison system's part in allowing two convicted murderers, two armed robbers, a child abuser, a burglar, and a serial rapist to escape.

"You don't have seven hardened criminals in an area where they don't belong, being guarded by one civilian officer," she said. "It's ludicrous to think they can't learn something from this."

"I think the elected officials of Texas are to blame," Mrs. Hawkins also said, this time to ABC News's *Good Morning America.* "I don't think they've watched the prison system." Hawkins said the events had devastated her family, especially her son's nine-year-old boy, Andrew.

"I was with him on Christmas morning," she said. "He changed his Santa Claus list, and said, 'I want Santa Claus to bring my daddy back.' " She said the child was undergoing grief counseling because of his father's murder.

"It's incumbent on us in his [Hawkins's] memory to go through with the responsibility and to fix whatever errors there were," said Glen Castlebury.

"Obviously, policies and procedures were not followed," said Mac Stringfellow, chairman of the TDCJ. "If those procedures are followed, an escape cannot occur, but when you get lax, this is what can result . . . the problem at the Connally Unit I certainly don't believe is systemic, but prudence requires that we take a look at the operation in all our prisons."

When the official report was finally released by the TDCJ on Thursday, January 11, 2001, it laid the blame, just as had been expected, on the prison staff rather than on the administration and the policies and procedures of the prison system. The report laid out a series of mistakes made by the correctional employees that led to the escape. Mistakes included those by staff members who failed to report unsupervised inmates and by guards who did not recognize inmates disguised as civilians. Also cited was the fire alarm, which was canceled by one officer Perez without being passed on to the prison's administrators. The report basically denied that staff shortages contributed to the escape.

"There is no evidence, no information, that the staffing situation contributed to this incident," said Gary Johnson, director of the prisons division of the TDCJ.

Stringfellow said that the escape was due in large part to correctional officer Lou Gips's failure to check the identification of an inmate disguised as a worker before letting him outside the compound and into a guard tower. That failure to follow prison policy was only one of several security breaches that occurred at the Connally Unit on the day of the escape, said Stringfellow, but it was one of the most significant breaches. If the correctional officer in question had only performed the identification check, one of the most rudimentary procedures, the inmates would have not been allowed out of the prison yard.

"We've got 30,000 correctional officers throughout Texas," Stringfellow said. "For the most part, everyone is hard-working, conscientious, and dedicated to their jobs. Because their jobs are so important, if they fail to follow procedures and guidelines, then this sort of thing can happen. That's where the problem lies."

At a meeting among prison officials when the report was released, guard Alejandro Marroquin, 23, threw his badge at one of the prison officials and quit his job on the spot when he was not allowed to ask questions concerning the report and the escape. He later went on *Good Morning America*, and said that prison officials had made him and others the scapegoats for the escape, adding that it appeared to him that the only way he could have avoided being blamed in the incident was by getting killed.

"They can take this job and shove it," Marroquin said after the meeting. "They're not paying us enough to risk our lives . . . they've got us between a rock and a hard place."

Marroquin told reporters that it was just a matter

of time before something like the escape happened, in part because of the administration's policies that allowed inmates to have access to tools.

Marroquin described for reporters and the national news media how he felt during the breakout and how close he believed he came to losing his life.

"Roughly about 11:45 we walked in, me and a fellow coworker, from lunch," Marroquin said. "I sat down like I normally do, went about my daily routine and noticed that all the inmates were coming out. They got into a conversation over some motor that they were talking about for a vacuum cleaner. Before I knew it, Rivas had come behind me and grabbed me. They had pulled the rolling chair from under me. I tried to fight for a while, but before I could they had possibly a ten-inch blade around my neck." He said that he was told, "If you're going to fight, you're going to die, and we will not hesitate to take your life."

"It they [the inmates] decide to turn on you at any specific second, there's nothing you can do," he said. "I tried to fight back, but after they're putting knives around your neck, you're not going to fight back. You know you're going to die, or you're going to live . . . nobody's going to risk their life. I mean I'm sorry for what happened to Mrs. Hawkins. Nobody can bring his life back, I understand that. But they're making it seem like if we would have put our lives on the line, his life would be back . . . they are trying to make the guards the scapegoats.

"I was the only guard," he continued. "Basically I

was not the security factor due to the fact that I was recruited to that position as a paint supervisor . . . I would detail the paint of the unit, paint where it was needed. I was never allowed to stay in that office as security. I was always sent to do other work. There were no correctional officers back there besides me."

Marroquin contended that the person or persons that should be blamed for the breakout were whoever was responsible for allowing the seven inmates to be in the maintenance department without adequate supervision.

"I think the station shouldn't have had those particular individuals in that area due to the fact that they had access to sensitive materials such as floor plans, screwdrivers, bolt cutters, stuff like that," Marroquin said. "They had planned this escape well and they executed it very well."

Jerry McDowell, the recreation specialist often referred to as the "Coach," was suspended following the board's findings. Afterward, McDowell, who had attended the same meeting that Marroquin had walked out of, said that he was unfairly suspended for not informing corrections officers that prisoners had congregated in the maintenance area which, he said, had a picniclike atmosphere in which inmates were being allowed to roam around unsupervised.

"That department is so wide open that inmates do what they like," McDowell told reporters. "It's like a park with picnics. To see an inmate unsupervised is not unusual . . . the atmosphere out there is so open, you have inmates running all around. It's changed since the breakout, but it was like that before."

McDowell, who had gone to the maintenance department to check out a toolbox, saw three inmates, including George Rivas, in the area. When he asked Rivas why they were there unsupervised, he claims that Rivas told him that Patrick Moczygemba, the maintenance supervisor, had left to run an errand at one of the prison dormitories. Because of the usual lax situation there, McDowell said that he accepted the explanation and left with the toolbox that he had borrowed. McDowell, who received a three-week suspension without pay and a year's probation over the incident, pointed out that he is paid less than correctional officers and has received no training in security procedures.

"My mind wasn't thinking about security," he said. "I'm not trained to do that. They are making it seem like a recreation specialist is responsible for the escape."

Larry Todd, spokesman for the TDJC, countered that McDowell's comments about lax security stood in contrast to claims made by prison officials who claimed that security at the Connally Unit was normally tight. Todd also questioned why McDowell didn't report his observations to his superiors.

"So, the question is, why didn't he do that?" Todd asked.

A sergeant at another maximum-security prison

who did not wish to be identified backed up McDowell's claims.

"They are not security staff," said the sergeant.

A former guard who asked for anonymity and had been beaten three times by Connally Unit inmates echoed similar feelings.

"Working there two and a half years, it didn't surprise me because while I was there I knew something was going to happen," said the guard. "Connally was an accident waiting to happen. I'm just glad I wasn't there when something did happen." The guard added that during his last year of employment at the Connally Unit, the prison was more than 80 guards short of the required staffing levels.

"I am still under the belief that lack of staffing is at the root of the problem," said Brian Olsen, deputy director of the American Federation of State, County and Municipal Employees. Although he conceded that guards made errors, he stated, "If it's a poorly run unit, the responsibility goes all the way up . . . someone has to take some responsibility, and I think it's at the Capitol."

"The system has failed, and it's our responsibility to discover how and why this failure occurred and take corrective action," said Gary Johnson.

"This report was designed to find out exactly what happened and what procedures were violated, what procedures were not followed and by whom," Mac Stringfellow said. "Obviously, we did have a breakdown in procedural compliance."

Corrections officer Randy Albert, who had been among the Texas 7's victims, voiced his opinion about the report from his home when he spoke to reporters. "Maybe there were things where policy wasn't followed, but it still goes back on the administration," Albert said, reiterating feelings that he had expressed earlier. "If you have people working for you and they're not doing their job and you just keep letting it happen, you're just as much at fault as those people working for you. They want to put it all on the officers, and that's fine, but those officers also answer to other people who are higher up."

Jayne Hawkins shot out at the board members and the State of Texas in voicing her dissatisfaction with the report.

"This report is ludicrous," she said. "It's a joke. You're using words like 'blame' and 'fault' when you should be talking about responsibility and accountability . . . without a good director you have a bad movie, and this is a tragic movie. You should all be embarrassed, you should be red-faced with shame."

Mrs. Hawkins said that this is what she expected, for the report to blame a small number of low-level employees while their superiors, the "higher-ups" in the prison system, would try to shake off responsibility.

"That's not to say that the prison workers involved shouldn't be held accountable for their mistakes during this escape," she said. "However, the Indians are only as good as the chiefs. I knew they'd try to blame this on two underpaid, undertrained, and overworked employees. Then they can fire two people and sigh and go on with business as usual.

"And [George W.] Bush can go to Washington and do the same thing for the country that he did for Texas.

"My child died," she continued. "I look at the criminals and I look at the board. They both pulled the trigger, in my opinion. I don't want an apology. I want change. That's what I demand in my son's honor."

In addition to the administrative actions against the employees named in the report, the prison board later demoted Connally Unit warden Timothy B. Keith.

In the aftermath of the breakout and her son's untimely death, Jayne Hawkins made it her goal to make changes within the prison system to prevent something like this from ever happening again. She has hired two lawyers to file a lawsuit against the state and the prison system. The lawsuit, she said, is not intended simply to win money but to bring effective changes to a system that has serious problems.

"I have no choice but to do this for Aubrey," she said. "He gave his life for justice. If change is accomplished, it will be in honor of Aubrey, and that's all I have left. His life will not have gone in vain . . . if

I can do something to make the world better, what else is there to do that makes sense? Aubrey wanted things to be better. He died trying to make things better."

CHAPTER

13

In most investigations of great intensity, such as those for murders or robberies, police officers and detectives generally begin a probe using standard investigative techniques. Prison breaks are no different. Utilizing such methods, the TDCJ investigators began their work at the Connally Unit by gathering as much information as they could about the escape of the Texas 7. They examined the crime scenes, what the escapees did to their victims, and made every effort to learn what they said to their victims. They examined the methods the escapees used in getting out of the prison, interviewed the guards who were known to be in regular contact with the escapees, and asked questions of the other inmates, particularly those that knew them.

They also examined the crime reports related to the offenses that landed the seven criminals in prison in the first place, to learn more about their individual methods of operation, to put together lists of all their known associates and family members on the outside. Then they interviewed those people, and looked at the prison's phone logs to determine who they had been in contact with recently. It was tedious work, but work that needed to be done to generate the kind of leads that could possibly set them on the path to learning where the elusive Texas 7 were hiding.

Much to their dismay, they learned that only one of the seven had been in contact with a relative in the not too distant past: Raul Rodriguez, 61, had recently visited his son, Michael. However, when the investigators contacted the father, he did not provide them with any information that could help them locate Michael or the others, or with anything else that might help them ascertain what the convicts' plans for the future might be. The last time the elder Rodriguez had seen or talked with his son was during the prison visit. Contacts with friends and relatives of all seven inmates also failed to yield any significant results.

One of the major problems hindering the investigation was the fact that the seven inmates had remained together since their escape. Historically, it was highly unusual for inmates to stick together. Normally when a group makes a break for it, they split up when they get on the outside, and one or more of them typically goes to see his family or prior known associates, making them easy for authorities to capture. When one is captured, investigators can often learn information from that inmate that will lead the cops to the others, usually one at a time. But since there was no apparent breakdown of the cohesiveness of this particular group of escapees, the investigative work was made all the more difficult. Results came in at a snail's pace, when at all.

Why had they remained together unlike so many others who had escaped from prison? The investigators kept asking themselves that question, as did an inquisitive and fascinated public.

They knew that the Texas 7 had committed at least two robberies and had murdered a police officer during one of them. The crimes had apparently created a solidifying effect within the group, or had at least reinforced one. They were in it together for the long haul, so to speak, and they were intelligent enough to realize that if they remained united their chances of getting caught were reduced. Each would also know what the others were doing at any given time and that would afford the smarter ones an opportunity to ward off acts of foolishness that might get them caught sooner rather than later.

Where were the escapees nearly a month after their carefully planned departure from the Connally Unit? Were they still in Texas, hunkered down somewhere and being helped by others? Or had they finally fled the state?

For now, despite an increase in the reward money

to $300,000, the only thing the investigators knew for certain was that they had no idea where the Texas 7 were hiding out.

"Traditionally, when an inmate escapes," said Jack Garner, a retired Texas prison warden, "they go to their momma, or their wife or girlfriend. We know that, and that's the first place we would go . . . In this case, it's obvious they're not going to momma's house."

At one point Clint Van Zandt, a former FBI profiler, was consulted. According to Van Zandt, it was not very likely that the escapees had traveled very far.

"Is this the type of group that would be hiding in Cleveland, Ohio?" he asked somewhat derisively at a news conference held to discuss possible locations where they might be hiding out. "I don't think so. They'll want to stay in their comfort zones, where they know the streets and the area and what the law enforcement presence is. They don't want to be the only Hispanic in Portland, Oregon."

With 25 years experience in tracking fugitives, Van Zandt offered some of his insight on this case.

"If their fantasy is continuing their life in another country, assuming another identity, they have to have funds to support their plan," Van Zandt said. "That means the group dynamic would be, 'We will stay together for a large financial score. We will stay together for the protection of the group. We will stay together so we won't be divided and conquered at this time. We will get the money we need, and at that point we'll break up into two or seven different groups and go our own way."

According to Van Zandt, the escapees were likely experiencing a great deal of stress relating to the Hawkins slaying and the increased public awareness and pressure on law enforcement agencies to bring the case to a conclusion. And it could have been even more stressful if one or more of them had been wounded during their attack on officer Hawkins. Keeping the group together, in Van Zandt's opinion, was likely not an easy task to accomplish.

"It takes one or more very strong people in leadership, and what you have to do is keep the group focused on their next objective," Van Zandt said.

"Given the antisocial personalities of these guys," he said, "they are going to become bored and need outside stimuli. They are going to be thinking that being in hiding is not much better than being in prison. They're going to be sitting around saying to themselves, 'Hell, this is as bad as prison. First, the authorities imprison us and, next, we imprison ourselves.' And how long they will go along with the self-imprisonment is only something that group can determine themselves.

"You've got a group of people with different desires, different drives, and different psychologies," Van Zandt continued. "One guy is going to want to go out for a steak dinner, another is going to want a new car, another to get together with a former girlfriend."

Van Zandt told *The Dallas Morning News* that if Rivas was indeed the leader like everyone believed, it was up to him to keep the group in line by maintaining strong, militarylike discipline. The leader or leaders would have to be able to convey to the rest of the group that they were all in it together, and that all of them were being hunted together under the threat of capital punishment if caught.

By this point in the investigation, not only were the Texas investigators frustrated over the lack of good, solid leads to point them to where the inmates might be holed up, but they had become concerned over the extensive media coverage the case had generated and they were worried that the attention might somehow serve to glorify the fugitives.

"Of course it's frustrating, but we've got to exercise patience and due diligence as we continue this massive manhunt," Larry Todd said. "We've also got to be careful to not place these escapees in the position of gaining notoriety. I heard some talk-show host compare them to Bonnie and Clyde and Jesse James. What a bunch of hogwash. These are cold-blooded killers who are mean as hell."

Todd also reiterated that his department and other law enforcement agencies involved in the manhunt were being careful about what and how much information they released to the public. While they would regularly share information that would help the public to identify the fugitives, they could not share specific details of the investigation or most of the tips that were called in.

"We know of at least two cases where news media attention prevented our investigation or a surveillance," Todd said. "I don't think there's anybody who would do anything to hurt our search, but we are having to be extremely cautious about what the police agencies are doing."

According to U.S. Marshall Dub Bransom, who had been working extensively on the investigation, everything that was being done was being done correctly. He stated that he had never seen a better-coordinated, more cooperative effort than that being conducted in the search for the Texas 7.

"You can rest well assured that everything, every possible means and everybody involved in this thing is making a maximum effort," Bransom told *The Dallas Morning News*. "Like they say in the old detective stories, 'We leave no stone unturned.' And that would exactly apply in this case. Right now, we're turning over the same stone a half-dozen times to make sure nothing's hung on the bottom."

Nonetheless, the authorities were frustrated at their seeming lack of progress in the case and at the fact that they kept coming up with zero nearly every time a viable sighting report came in. Another point of frustration was the fact that, despite the large reward for the Texas 7, there had so far been no takers. One investigator said that he had seen mothers sell their sons for considerably less than $300,000.

"We ought to be able to find the shooter on the grassy knoll for that kind of money," said an official.

As the manhunt continued, one lead that came in that looked good placed two of the Texas 7, Randy Halprin and Donald Newbury, at an Exxon gas station approximately 74 miles north of Houston on Monday, January 15. A clerk at the station, located on Highway 105 near Navasota, Texas, called the local police shortly after 11 A.M. and reported that two of the seven had just left the station driving in a red flatbed truck along with several other men.

When the police arrived, the clerk told them that the two men entered the store portion of the station. One of them went to the food counter, and the other lingered about trying on sunglasses. They attempted to use a credit card that was either not valid or was over the limit, and asked for directions to Conroe, Texas, a small town some 30 miles east of Navasota. After being shown photographs of the seven suspects, the clerks identified Halprin and Newbury as the men who had come into the store. Despite putting out an all-points bulletin, the police were unable to locate any vehicles matching the description given to them by the clerks.

A surveillance tape was obtained from the store and was sent to the Texas Department of Corrections in Huntsville to be reviewed, but the quality of the images was too poor to make an identification of the two men. The tape was then forwarded to a lab at Sam Houston University in Huntsville where attempts were made to enhance the imagery of the tape, to no avail. Fingerprint samples left by the two men on paper at the store, as well as fingerprints lifted from a number of locations inside and outside the store, failed to identify the suspects as well. When all was said and done, investigators discounted the latest possible sighting, and said that the two men were likely not two of the seven fugitives.

In the meantime the reward money was increased again. That same day, January 15, the FBI kicked in $140,000 of its own money to bring the reward total to $440,000. By the end of the week, the Bureau of Alcohol, Tobacco and Firearms donated $60,000 to the cause, which increased the reward total to $500,000.

By the time the reward money had reached a half-million dollars, bounty hunters in search of the Texas 7 seemed to begin coming out of the woodwork, bringing with them more concern—particularly for public safety—to the official investigators working on the case. Bounty hunters, who normally make their money by tracking down suspects who jump bail, are required to hold a private investigator's license to work in Texas. However, under Texas requirements, such a license is not needed when the people being hunted are prison escapees. Some of the bounty hunters wanted the big payoff of the reward money, while others claimed they just wanted to do their part to get the seven fugitives off the streets and back behind bars where they belong. The official investigators, however, were worried that the bounty hunters might get in the way, or that someone, particularly a civilian, might inadvertently get hurt or killed.

Citing the viciousness that the Texas 7 exhibited in their assassination of Aubrey Hawkins, Texas police officials issued stern warnings that civilians should stay clear of the fugitives, for their own safety. They warned that it would be in everyone's best interest if the matter were left in the hands of law enforcement. They did, however, encourage any of the bounty hunters with legitimate tips to contact one of the many hotlines available, or to simply call their local police department.

Another concern for the manhunters, especially the official ones, was George Rivas himself. Previously characterized as "the most dangerous man in El Paso," the investigators believed that he was the type of person who would never give up. The facts that he was brighter than most of the people he led or associated with, and that he always seemed to have a plan of action, say the authorities, were what made him particularly dangerous. He had developed a plan to escape from the Connally Unit that was ingenious enough to get the others to follow him out, successfully, and the law officers figured that with all of the firepower he and the others had stockpiled, he likely had a contingency plan for the confrontation that he knew would be inevitable. Charged with capital murder, threatened with penalty of death, Rivas would likely figure that he had nothing to lose and would be willing to go out—taking the others with him—in a blaze of glory.

For now, despite the hundreds of leads and dozens of false alarms, no one had a clue about the fugitives' whereabouts.

CHAPTER
14

As the search for the Texas 7 continued, *America's Most Wanted* ran a segment on the elusive fugitives on Saturday, January 20, the third such airing about the case on that program. The program basically reiterated what was known about the seven escapees, and provided information about what was now a $500,000 reward in the hope that it would bring forward someone who had seen the convicts or knew where they were hiding.

In the meantime the sightings, real or imagined, continued. A gas station clerk in Fillmore, Utah, located just off Interstate 15, about halfway between St. George and Salt Lake City, reported three customers that he suspected of being part of the gang. He wrote down the license plate number of the van they were driving, and the police set up roadblocks in the vicinity. Before long they stopped the van with the matching plate. It turned out that the men in the van were not the escapees.

Within the same time frame, two separate tipsters, unknown to each other, reported seeing Patrick Murphy, Jr. at a home in Jackson, Mississippi that was believed to have been owned by one of Murphy's relatives. The lead seemed especially credible, prompting the FBI to set up a stakeout of the house. Again, however, it turned out to be a false lead. The house had nothing to do with Murphy or his relatives, and the man who had been seen coming and going from it was not Murphy.

The elusiveness of the Texas 7 not only continued to bewilder the investigators in all of the different agencies working on the case, it also increased the fear surrounding the fugitives. They were supposedly being seen everywhere—even New York City—and the sightings were beginning to hint at mass hysteria, something the investigators did not need.

"This is an incredibly difficult case," said John F. Clark of the U.S. Marshals Service. "It's one unlike any I've ever seen. To this point, we're just stymied." They were baffled despite having more than two dozen officers working on the case from that agency alone.

Although officials from virtually every agency working on the case admitted their frustration at the lack of progress, all of them denied that the search effort was at a dead end. They held out hope that the huge reward would eventually bring them the desired results. The FBI's huge contribution of $140,000 to the reward fund was out of the ordinary, as the agency rarely puts up that kind of money.

"It's very unusual," said Special Agent Lori Bailey, spokesperson for the FBI's Dallas office. "That we are contributing is indicative of our commitment to finding these guys ... it's a lot of money. These aren't ghosts. Someone out there knows where they are."

"I think people are constantly aware of these guys," said David Tull of the Irving Police Department. "Nobody wants them driving up next to them. There's such a public interest in them being caught because they are dangerous and vicious and are already proven cop killers."

At one point the magnitude of the Texas 7 case was compared to that of the so-called "Railroad Murderer," Angel Maturino Resendez. In that case the suspect's family proved instrumental in bringing it to a successful conclusion, and the investigators hunting for the Texas 7 hoped for something similar in their case.

Although the investigators didn't know it yet, they were about to get what they were hoping for, except it would not be a relative of any of the Texas 7 who helped them. Wade Holder, owner of the Coachlight RV Park in Woodland Park, Colorado, located a few miles northwest of Colorado Springs and near the

U.S. Air Force Academy, had watched *America's Most Wanted* on Saturday night and thought that he recognized some of the fugitives. A group of seven men had checked into the park on Monday, January 1, driving a 32-foot Pace Arrow RV and other vehicles. They had told him that they were traveling Christians doing missionary work, and they seemed like such a nice, pleasant group of men. One of them had even joined a small Bible study group at the park within days of their arrival. But Holder became suspicious after seeing the latest installment of *America's Most Wanted*, and his suspicions had bothered him all night long. He wanted to make the call to the police, but he also wanted to be certain that his suspicions were correct. To be sure that he wasn't making a mistake, he fired up his computer the next day and checked out the mug shots of the Texas 7 on AMW's Web site. After viewing the photos for a while, there was no longer any doubt in his mind. The Texas 7 were indeed staying at his park. Astounded by what he had discovered, he didn't know what to do. If things weren't handled properly and carefully, it could get dangerous really fast, not only for him but also for others staying in the park. But he knew that he had to do the right thing.

Woodland Park, Colorado, is located on a high, broad plateau, 8,500 feet above sea level. Situated on the north slope of Pike's Peak, it takes its name from the thickly wooded hills and valleys surrounding it. It

sits near Ute Pass, giving easy access to Colorado
Springs to the east, Denver to the north, and a number
of mountain recreation areas in just about any direc-
tion. Mountain lakes and streams are abundant, as are
the trout, making it a fisherman's heaven. Hiking,
back-packing, camping, cycling, horseback riding and
a number of other recreational activities make it a
particularly fun place for the outdoors types in the
summer months, and in the winter, locals and visitors
alike enjoy cross-country skiing, snowmobiling,
snowshoeing, ice fishing, and ice skating. These recreational activities, the fresh crisp air, and the lack of
congestion had prompted Wade Holder and others to
settle here. To the investigators working on the Texas
7 case, it seemed like an unlikely place for a group
of dangerous fugitives to bed down. But that's what
they did. Investigators would later consider it amazing
that they had gone unnoticed for over three weeks,
before Wade Holder finally recognized them.

Shortly after four P.M. on Sunday, January 21,
Holder called 911 and reported his suspicions to Teller County Sheriff's Department Deputy Nicholas Pinell, and from there the case broke wide open.

CHAPTER

15

Immediately after receiving the tip about the Texas 7 from Wade Holder, Deputy Nicholas Pinell called his superior, Sergeant Bud Bright, at home. It was Bright's day off, but he took the call. Astounded at what Pinell had told him, Bright called Sheriff Frank Fehn and the three of them agreed to meet in an hour. Fehn, 72, a retired detective from New York who had investigated 385 homicides, was anxious to get the operation underway.

Following additional conversations with Holder, who told the sheriff that one of the men had two front teeth missing and had complained to him that he was wearing a dental plate that was causing him pain, Fehn called the U.S. Marshals office in Denver, which in turn contacted the Texas 7 command post in Huntsville, Texas. That group was set up in a facility near the state's execution chamber some 1,057 or so miles south of Woodland Park, Colorado. Fehn and the other investigators subsequently learned that one of the escapees had left a dental plate behind at the prison during the escape, and one of the other escapees had regularly quoted Scripture to the other inmates. The tip that Holder had given them now seemed more viable than ever. They just hoped that the tip didn't turn out to be another dead end, like so many of the others. They didn't waste any time in putting together a plan of action to capture the fugitives if it turned out that they were, in fact, holed up at the RV park.

January 21, 2001 was a dark, overcast night. The cloud cover would likely bring more snow to the area overnight. At approximately 10 P.M. Fehn and Bright took an unmarked car and drove to within 50 yards of the recreational vehicle that they believed was being used by the Texas 7, to scope out the situation from a law enforcement standpoint. It was a picturesque setting in daylight hours, with Pikes Peak nearby and the RV park surrounded by ponderosa pine trees, not the sort of place they would have expected seven hardened criminals and now, cop killers, to be hiding out. But now, the setting was almost ideal for the escaped convicts. Fehn's first concern was how they were going to approach the situation from a strategic perspective and not get anyone hurt or killed in the process. There was going to be substantial risk to life and property, and he knew it.

Meanwhile, Ron Knight, 51, the violent crimes supervisor for the FBI in Denver, had gone to bed after being briefed and learning that Sheriff Fehn, with help from FBI field agents, was working on attempting to eliminate the men inside the RV as suspects. One of Knight's agents woke him up three hours later and informed him that because of the potential danger to civilians, as well as to law enforcement officers, it would not be tactically feasible to attempt to flush out the suspects in the present setting. There were far too many motor homes with people inside them in close proximity to the suspected RV to risk such an action. As a result, it would not be possible confirm that the men inside the Pace Arrow were the men that they were looking for. The investigators had also learned that the men drove two other vehicles in and out of the RV park. One was a brown Ford van, and the other a silver Jeep Cherokee.

Knight didn't waste any time. He got dressed, grabbed his file on the Texas 7 and left his Littleton, Colorado home and began the hour-and-a-half drive to the Teller County Sheriff's Department.

When Knight arrived at about four A.M., a total of seven officers from the U.S. Marshal's office, FBI, Teller County Sheriff's Department, and the neighboring El Paso County Sheriff's Department filled Sheriff Fehn's small, unassuming office to begin making plans on how they were going to deal with the

seven men in the RV. Knight had been an Army
Ranger in Vietnam, and he had led SWAT team operations during standoffs with David Koresh and his
Branch Davidian religious followers at Waco, with the
Freemen in Montana, and at the Ruby Ridge home-
stead of Randy and Vicki Weaver in Idaho, which
resulted in the deaths of Vicki and their son, Sammy.
The group selected Knight as the person in charge of
this operation.

After the group of investigators had collected all of
the information regarding how the Texas 7 had arrived in Woodland Park and attempted to blend into
the community, they found it all a little perplexing,
even fantastic. While it seemed like it had been a
smart move for all of the seven fugitives to have arrived together under the guise of traveling Christians,
it could also have been their undoing. Most of the
nation's eyes were on the lookout for seven men traveling together. The investigators found themselves
wondering why the fugitives had taken that chance
when they could have arrived separately, in groups of
twos or threes, spacing their arrivals apart by several
hours or even a couple of days. That seemed like it
would have been a safer plan and it likely would have
drawn less attention to themselves.

They had already shown that those trying to profile
them weren't one hundred percent correct in their as-
sessments: They had traveled out of their so-called
comfort zones. But whether their arriving together at
the Coachlight RV Park had been a smart move or a

dumb one, they had pulled it off by remaining united. If anyone had noticed them or had suspected that they were the Texas outlaws, they may have set their suspicions aside after learning what a nice bunch of fellows they now had as neighbors. If not for *America's Most Wanted*, the Texas 7 might have gone unnoticed for months to come.

As Monday morning, January 22, wore on, Knight asked the group who would be willing to volunteer to conduct a mobile assault. In this instance, that would mean a police assault operation on a moving vehicle, if such an operation became necessary. Without hesitation, El Paso County Undersheriff Donald Kessler volunteered the group of men he would be leading. Kessler rounded up eight SWAT team members and directed them in practice sessions in the parking lot behind the sheriff's office.

It was also decided that all radio communications involving the operation would be cut off. The investigators were aware of the police scanners that the inmates had stolen during their robbery of the Radio Shack in Pearland, and they did not want to take any chances that the seven were listening in. Even though they would have had to have obtained new frequencies for the scanners after their arrival in Colorado, frequencies for police scanners were public information in most states and not that difficult to obtain. Just to play it safe, radios were definitely out. They would use cellular telephones instead. However, due to the mountainous terrain that often resulted in poor signals in the area, the use of the phones would be limited and their effectiveness would ultimately prove to be less than optimum during the operation.

Next on their agenda was to develop a plan in which they could move the SWAT teams into the RV park without being noticed. Sheriff Fehn told the group that he owned an RV, and offered its use. He volunteered to pose as a tourist, change the license plate to an out-of-state plate, and drive the teams in. When the group agreed to the plan, ten SWAT team members from the FBI practiced the planned mobilization, particularly getting in and out of Fehn's RV quickly while carrying automatic assault rifles and wearing body armor. They appropriately code-named Fehn's RV, "The Trojan Horse."

Shortly after dawn, after the operation had begun but before the assault teams were ready to move into place, Knight's cellular phone rang. One of his agents informed him that the brown Ford van was gone from where it had been parked earlier. One or more of the men had driven it out of the park before the SWAT teams could secure the park's perimeter. The operation had suddenly become more difficult, and potentially more dangerous. Instead of keeping the park's perimeter secure, they had to worry about when the van, carrying an undetermined number of people, might return and catch the cops as they moved into their positions.

Their tipster, Wade Holder, previously told the investigators about the almost-daily routine of the seven men from the Pace Arrow RV: Nearly every morning, they either walked or drove down the hill to the office for coffee and conversation. Knight's plan was to be in place, waiting on them so that they could use the element of surprise when they walked into the office. Despite the current problem involving the missing brown Ford van, five members of an FBI SWAT team had managed to take up positions inside the RV park's office after climbing out of Sheriff Fehn's "Trojan Horse," which was parked just outside. Five other SWAT team members remained inside the RV. Fehn, donning a bulletproof vest concealed beneath a shirt and a blue jacket that helped to ease the winter chill, lingered around the office pretending that he was a tourist, waiting to check into the park and receive a parking spot for his RV.

Police sharp shooters took their positions at the top of a hill, above the RV where they believed the Texas 7 were hiding out. Just when everyone thought that matters couldn't get any worse, they did. Three men came out of the RV and hopped into the silver Jeep Cherokee parked nearby. Fehn, several hundred feet down the hill, had been notified of the suspects' movement and climbed quickly back inside his own RV to await their arrival. However, instead of stopping at the office, they drove right by everyone, out of the park, and turned west onto U.S. Highway 24.

The El Paso County Sheriff's Department's SWAT team, the group that had volunteered to conduct the assault on a moving vehicle if necessary, was ready. They followed several blocks behind the silver Cherokee in a black van and a white Chevrolet Tahoe sport utility vehicle. Soon after entering Woodland Park, and to everyone's horror, the Cherokee turned into the parking lot of a Safeway grocery store, the site where the authorities had set up the communications outpost for their operation! They could only hope that the suspects didn't go anywhere near the rear of the store where the outpost, which consisted of a clearly marked El Paso County Sheriff's Department van and other marked vehicles, was partially hidden from view. No one had planned for this contingency, and everyone only hoped and prayed that the men in the Cherokee didn't spot that arm of the operation. If they did, the situation could turn deadly very quickly, particularly with all of the people who steadily came and went from the store and with the steady stream of customers going in and out of the adjacent Burger King.

El Paso County Sheriff John Anderson watched the Cherokee and its occupants from a safe distance. The driver got out and went into the store and the other two men remained inside the vehicle. Anderson repeatedly tried to reach his colleagues on his cellular phone, but he couldn't get a signal to place the call. Dressed in civilian clothes, Anderson got out of his vehicle and walked into the parking lot to attempt to get a closer look. As he did so, the driver came out of the store and got back inside the Cherokee and drove away.

One of the SWAT team members finally got his phone to work, and he relayed the message that the Cherokee was traveling on U.S. Highway 24 again, this time heading east. The message was relayed to El Paso County Sheriff's Department SWAT team commander Terry Maketa, who in turn relayed it to Lieutenant Ken Moore, who began looking for the silver Cherokee farther down the highway. Thankful that the Cherokee had left the site of the busy store, the vehicle assault team continued their pursuit from a safe distance. Anderson was two cars behind the Cherokee, as were the SWAT team vehicles, when it turned into the Western convenience store and gas station and parked next to a gas pump.

In a somewhat spur-of-the-moment but fully coordinated effort, Maketa pulled his car in front of the Cherokee to block it from moving forward, and the van carrying the vehicle assault SWAT team members pulled in behind the Cherokee. Six SWAT team members jumped out of the van and trained their automatic assault rifles on the three suspects, sending horrified customers screaming and running away from the scene.

"Get your hands in the air!" shouted one of the cops.

"Don't move!" shouted another. "Get your hands up!"

Without taking their eyes off of the three men for even a second, the SWAT team advanced toward the Cherokee, their guns pointed and ready to shoot in an instant if any one of the three suspects made a move that the police perceived as threatening. One of the cops pulled the driver out of the Cherokee first and threw him onto the pavement, while another searched the fanny pack he was wearing. Not surprisingly, the fanny pack contained a handgun. The lawmen immediately recognized the driver as Joseph Garcia.

Michael Rodriguez was in the back seat, also wearing a fanny pack. When the cops pulled him out of the Cherokee, a handgun fell and landed on the pavement with several frightening clanks. One of the SWAT team members kicked it out of the way while another one frisked Rodriguez, finding another handgun in his fanny pack in the process.

George Rivas was the passenger in the front seat. As he got out of the vehicle, one of the cops continuously yelled at him to keep his hands where they could be seen. Rivas stopped and glared at the police officers, and at one point his fingers began to twitch, as if he might have been considering making a break for it. For all the cops knew, he might have been planning to reach for yet another gun that they hadn't seen yet. For several moments it was tense for everyone concerned as they waited to see whether Rivas was going to go peacefully or if he was going to opt for a deadly shootout. Finally, after realizing that there was no possible chance of escaping with his life, Rivas relented. After being forced to remove their shirts, each man was handcuffed and placed inside

separate patrol cars and driven to the Teller County
Jail.

With three down and four to go, the cops knew
they still had their work cut out for them. They didn't
know where the brown Ford van was or who was
driving it, and they didn't know which, if any, of the
seven were still at the RV park.

That changed rapidly, however, when the local police intercepted a cellular phone call shortly after Rivas, Rodriguez, and Garcia were arrested. Roadblocks
had been set up along the highway near the RV park.
The call was clearly a tip-off, a warning to one or
more of the remaining fugitives.

The caller said, "They're searching cars, and they
might be on to you."

At that point the police did not know to whom the
call had been placed, or by whom. Although attempts
were made to identify the caller and his or her location, the effort failed because of the large number of
motorists who had been stopped as a result of the
roadblock, many of whom were using their cellular
phones at the time. They were reasonably certain,
however, that the call had come from a car near the
roadblock.

CHAPTER

16

Well aware that they had lost the element of surprise in apprehending the remaining fugitives, Sheriff Frank Fehn crammed as many SWAT team members as he could into his Trojan Horse and returned to the Coachlight RV Park. He stopped approximately 50 yards from the Pace Arrow to await further instructions. Six snipers had taken up positions on a ridge southeast of the RV while additional SWAT personnel secured the areas to the north and west of it. They would attempt to enforce a 360-degree perimeter around the RV.

One of the occupants of a motor home adjacent to the suspects' RV saw the police activity, and all of the guns aimed toward the Pace Arrow. Terrified, she grabbed her young son and daughter and took them inside, placing them inside a closet, fearful that some of the flying bullets might pierce the thin walls of her trailer if gunfire broke out. Less than half an hour later, sheriff's deputies brought the woman and her children out of the motor home and took them to a safe location. The standoff continued.

With the prior radio silence now broken, the police radios crackled.

"There's someone with a long gun moving inside the RV!" reported one of the snipers on a nearby ridge.

"Give them every opportunity to surrender," barked Mark Mershon, the FBI agent in charge who had just arrived on the scene. "Let's try to negotiate them out."

Minutes later, Mershon stationed Special Agent Mark Holstlaw outside the RV with a bullhorn in his hand.

"You are completely surrounded," Holstlaw said, his voice echoing through the forest. "Come out with your hands in the air!"

One of the occupants in the RV went to a window and peered out momentarily, then quickly disappeared from sight. Moments later the door of the RV opened slowly, and a man walked out, his hands high in the air. He was wearing a shoe on one foot and a sandal on the other. It was Randy Halprin.

"I'm hurt," Halprin shouted to the police officers. "I've been shot in my foot. I'm hurt."

When Halprin had moved a reasonably safe distance from the trailer, the cops rushed him and took him into custody. After frisking him and handcuffing him, they took him to a location down the road and questioned him.

Halprin told the agents that Larry Harper was still inside, armed with rifles, handguns, shotguns, and a cache of ammunition. At least one of the rifles was a Colt AR-15 assault weapon that had been taken during their breakout at the prison, and it greatly concerned the cops. It had the ability to pierce the bulletproof vests that they were wearing.

Harper, the convicted rapist, wanted to talk to his father, Halprin told the cops. After discussing the issue among themselves, the lawmen agreed to the request and U.S. Marshal Girard McCann telephoned the Texas 7 command post in Huntsville as the first step in trying to locate Harper's father. While his father was being tracked down, Agent Holstlaw got on the bullhorn and informed Harper of their agreement.

"We'll let you talk to your father," Holstlaw said. "Everyone is in custody. Come out and we'll let you talk to your father."

There was no response from the Pace Arrow. Instead, several minutes later, at approximately 12:45 P.M., the sound of a muffled shot came from inside the RV. The SWAT teams recognized it as a gunshot; some of the other officers thought that Harper had kicked the inside wall of the RV. A few minutes later, the snipers again detected movement from inside the trailer. At one P.M. another gunshot, more distinct than the first, resounded from inside the trailer. Afterward, there were no further signs of movement.

Knight and Mershon, thinking that perhaps Harper had committed suicide, discussed the possibility of sending someone inside. Knight, however, was reluctant. It could, after all, be a trick, and he did not want to risk anyone's life by putting them up against an AR-15. They decided to wait.

Holstlaw made several attempts with the bullhorn to get a response from Harper. But there were no responses from inside. Over the next hour, the snipers on the hillsides thought that they had detected slight signs of movement inside the trailer. However, they considered that it might have only been sunlight and shadows on the blinds, cast by the pine trees moving in the wind. Finally, FBI SWAT team leader Mike Castro told Knight that he wanted to use tear gas.

FBI sniper Scott Doner, positioned on one of the ridges, fired three canisters of tear gas into the trailer through one of its windows. Everything remained still, with no movement detected inside.

"Come out, it's not too late," Holstlaw said through the bullhorn. "We don't want you to get hurt." Still there was no response.

Knight and Mershon decided that it was time to make the next move. Just down the hill a bit, FBI agents prepared a SWAT vehicle with two bullet shields on the front, and swathed the vehicle's hood area and windshield with blankets made out of bulletproof Kevlar material. Special Agent John Gedney volunteered to drive the vehicle toward the Pace Arrow. Peering through the two-inch slit in the bullet shields, Gedney drove slowly up the hill toward the RV. Four SWAT members walked closely behind the vehicle.

When they were positioned in close proximity to the trailer, they tossed a "flash-bang" explosive device—designed to cause disorientation—into the trailer through a window. Like before with the tear gas, there was no response and no movement from inside. Special Agent Rich Price, wearing body armor and a gas mask, hurriedly approached the trailer's door with a large tool, called a Halligan, capable of prying it open. After several quick attempts, Price was able to force the door open.

Knight and agent Dale Monroe rushed inside, toward the driver's area, while Castro and agent Rich Gill went to the rear of the trailer. Castro loudly called out that he had found Harper.

"I think he's dead!" Castro said.

They found Larry Harper lying on his back, on top of two handguns, with a large bloodstain on his chest that had trickled into a pool on the floor next to his body. There were two obvious shots to his heart. They reasoned that he had died slowly after having shot himself twice. The first shot had only wounded him, but the second shot, nearly fifteen minutes later, had finished him off. Not taking any chances, the agents handcuffed the body.

They found a suicide note in the bathroom, addressed to Harper's mother and father. It was lying on top of a Bible.

With five down and two to go, Knight and the rest of the investigative team began planning their next move. They now knew that Patrick Murphy and Donald Newbury, the only ones left, had taken the brown Ford van. Now all they had to do was find them.

CHAPTER

17

Many of the 8,000 residents of the sleepy little mountain town of Woodland Park, Colorado, nestled in the Pike National Forest and known by the locals as "the City Above the Clouds," were stunned that their town had been home for at least three weeks to the most hunted fugitives in the country. They were equally shocked that their town had been the setting for the dramatic capture of four of the Texas 7 and the suicide of a fifth. They only hoped that the remaining two fugitives were far away from their normally peaceful community.

The place was still buzzing with police activity, however, as a dragnet for Newbury and Murphy got underway and as agents interviewed the residents of the Coachlight Motel and RV Park to learn additional information.

One female resident described the fugitives as very polite and nice fellows who she would never have suspected as cop killers and escaped convicts. They were always well dressed and friendly and, except for the loud religious music that they often played in their motor home, were usually very quiet.

Sammi McCombs, 50, the assistant manager of the Western Gas and Convenience Store in town, told police that Rivas, Rodriguez, and Garcia came into the store almost every morning between 6:30 and seven for coffee and pastries. On one occasion all seven of them came into the store together, and she said that she thought they were part of a work crew of some kind heading out to their jobs. She thought that the blond-haired Rivas, who was always the best dressed, was their boss. He always seemed in charge and always paid for their food. He often conversed with her, mostly making small talk, but never saying anything about any of the others. She said they never seemed threatening and appeared quite ordinary.

"At any time they could have done anything to us," McCombs said in retrospect.

Wade Holder, manager of the Coachlight RV Park, told the investigators that the fugitives told him upon their arrival that they were traveling Christians, on their way to California. Having no reason to disbelieve them, Holder invited them to the weekly Bible-study group that he and his wife, Gina, had been holding at the park for quite some time.

Holder told the investigators that even though something bothered him about the seven men in the RV, he couldn't quite put his finger on it. Holder, himself deeply religious, said that it was their seemingly normal and low-key lifestyles, and especially Larry Harper's strong knowledge of the Bible, that had ultimately convinced him they were who they claimed to be.

"Harper was incredibly knowledgeable of the Bible," Holder said. "I think the man was a saved man . . . he asked me in one of the Bible study meetings to be forgiven for all he'd ever done wrong to anybody." Holder added that Harper had not confessed anything specific.

Rod Porteous, 50, a resident of Palm Springs, California, had been temporarily living at the park and told the police that he met Larry Harper at the Bible-study class. He went by the name of Jim, and, through his participation in the class and his knowledge of the Bible, he had impressed many of the others in the group. He occasionally took some of the study group members to lunch and paid the tab.

"He seemed to know the Bible," Porteous said. "He knew the Scriptures to quote, and he seemed to know the subject we were talking about, Matthew 13, so I would never have imagined that he was part of that group."

Most of the people investigators interviewed at the

Coachlight RV Park told them that they had believed the fugitives' story of being Christian missionaries on their way to California, although their actions sometimes seemed to contradict what they wanted people to believe. For example, their consumption of beer ran quite heavy at times, according to some of the residents, and all of them smoked cigarettes.

"There were always a lot of people coming over there," said one local resident who lived near the fugitives' last campsite. "They got kind of noisy at night. They all smoked."

According to what the investigators were being told, it was Harper's behavior that appeared to keep everyone's suspicions at bay.

"He was very soft spoken, very gentle," Holder said.

Another resident, Karen Schleuter, had been impressed by his knowledge of the Bible, and the fact that he could quote, in Hebrew, Christ's last words as he hung on the cross.

"He made your mind hungry for knowledge," Schleuter said.

The investigators learned that a number of women in the Bible study group had attempted to set up Harper on a date with a women near his age, but later, after finding out about his conviction for aggravated sexual assault, they were grateful that their attempts had been unsuccessful. No one had observed anything sexually aberrant about him.

Colorado Springs is known as a center for conservative Christianity, and is home to numerous Christian talk radio stations. "We get Christian groups coming through here all the time," Holder said. "We must get 40 new faces a month."

Despite their supposed Christian background, Holder told investigators, something about the men had bothered him. In retrospect, he said that he must have seen their mug shots on television.

"But I kind of blew it off and wasn't paying good attention then," he said. He said that he later had mentioned his uneasiness about the Texas 7 case to a friend, before he realized that the fugitives were in fact his "Christian" tenants. "I said, 'Wouldn't it be weird if they showed up here?' "

On a typical day they'd go shopping at Wal-Mart or Safeway, Holder told the cops. "They'd come in and out at various times, just like anyone else."

Although there was considerable snow and ice on the roads at that time of the year, Holder told the investigators that the fugitives did not appear to have any difficulty driving in it. Their brown Ford van was equipped with four-wheel drive, and they moved their RV several times during their three-week stay at the park. Each time they moved it, Holder said on retrospect, they moved it to a more remote location of the park. They paid $125 a week for their rental space, and they always paid in cash.

Darby Howard, 48, owner of Tres Hombres, one of Woodland Park's Mexican restaurants, said that the fugitives came in often and had commented that his establishment was one of their favorite places to go. They would come in for lunch and sometimes dinner, drink beer and shoot pool in his bar, but they were always quiet and respectful.

"They were always quiet and never started any trouble or drew attention to themselves," Howard said. "All we remember is that they drank Shiner beer." Although he never suspected them of being the Texas 7, Howard said that after the arrests he felt like he had just missed out on the Texas lottery.

When they came into the Tres Hombres to eat, drink, and play pool—two of them would often wear cowboy hats—no one thought anything unusual about them. One local thought that a couple of the fugitives were cadets from the Air Force Academy, while others noticed Donald Newbury's lizard tattoo near his neck but thought nothing of it at the time. They normally just sat by the fireplace near the entrance and spoke softly to each other, out of earshot of the other patrons.

"Just about everybody here remembers seeing the guy with the lizard tattoo," said Tres Hombres co-owner Sandy Ullom, "but everybody here has tattoos. Everybody up here is so weird you just blend in."

In their search for any prior connections that the fugitives might have had to the community, the investigators turned up nothing. The only thing that connected any one of them to Colorado at all was a skiing trip to Vail that Michael Rodriguez had taken in 1995, about a week before he pleaded guilty to capital murder in the murder-for-hire death of his wife.

As the search for Donald Newbury and Patrick Murphy, Jr. continued, the fugitives' own families helped characterize them for the public, as well as the police. Newbury's wife, Jacqueline, publicly stated that she was still in love with her husband and that she had been praying for his safety. She said that she was not aware of how her husband became involved with the other inmates, but believed that he joined up with them so that he could see his family.

"Day and night I think about it," she said. "I have nightmares . . . yeah, he committed a robbery, but nobody was ever killed. I'm not afraid of my husband. He's never hurt me or my family. I know my husband, and I know he would never harm anybody." She stated that he was good to her and the five children she had from prior relationships, but that she had not seen him for approximately a year.

"I'm sure he still loves me, and I love him, too," she said.

Newbury's court-appointed attorney, Kent Anschutz, who represented him in his earlier criminal proceedings, told the *Dallas Morning News* that Newbury's background indicated that he had positive qualities.

"All I can tell you is that from my knowledge of Donald's history," Anschutz told a reporter, "he never hurt, physically hurt, anyone. I wouldn't be surprised at anything when you have five to seven armed desperate men, but my honest gut reaction is that I would be very doubtful that he was a shooter in that (Oshman's) incident."

Murphy's relatives, on the other hand, expressed fears after the Oshman's robbery that he would hurt someone else.

"Patrick is the kind of guy who's going to fight to the very end," said Bruce White, one of his uncles. "That's just his style." According to White, Murphy had begun talking to relatives about coming to live with them if he made the parole that he would have soon been eligible for, but they told him that they didn't want him living with them because of their young children. "I think that kind of set him off."

Murphy, who had served the longest amount of time of the seven fugitives, but was the only one coming up for parole, had not been in touch with his uncle since shortly after being sent to prison in 1984. Murphy's religious beliefs were based on Odinism, a religion centered on the mythological god of war, Odin, and they stated that death during battle was considered the greatest reward. White said that Murphy was a man of violence obsessed with sex.

"When someone turns him down [for sex]," White said, "he gets very hostile." Although Murphy had admitted raping his former classmate, he had remained angry over the years because she had turned him in for the crime.

"I think he's a psycho," White said. "You just don't take somebody's life, especially when they have kids," he said to Hawkins's slaying. "If I could see Patrick, I'd shoot him myself."

Among the seven convicts, the investigators believed that Murphy, the sex offender, might be the weak link in the group. They believed he might succumb to his deviant sexual urges and get caught doing it. They only hoped that they could find him before that happened.

Meanwhile, on Tuesday morning, January 23, Woodland Park resident Wilma David was driving to work in nearby Colorado Springs just before dawn when she heard a news report on the radio that the police were looking for a brown Ford van they believed was connected to the Texas 7. Thinking little about it, she pulled into the parking lot of the Hungry Farmer restaurant where she normally stopped for breakfast. As she got out of her car she saw, much to her surprise, a brown Ford van parked there. It matched the description of the one that she had just heard about on the radio. After going inside the restaurant, she called the police.

When the police arrived, they had no trouble identifying the van. The license plate matched the number they had. When they looked inside they found that the keys were still in the ignition, and they found two boxes of men's hair dye on the floor.

The call went out that the van had been identified

and, because there was a Quality Inn motel next door that shared the parking lot with the restaurant, additional manpower was ordered to the scene. Within the hour the place was literally crawling with law enforcement personnel from all of the agencies involved in the manhunt. The adjacent streets were sealed off, the motel's guests were evacuated, and police armed to the hilt conducted a room-by-room search. However, when all was said and done, there was no sign of Patrick Murphy, Jr. and Donald Newbury. Mark Mershon, however, believed that they were close to nabbing the fugitives and said that it would only be a matter of time before they were found.

Mershon couldn't have been more correct. Shortly before nine P.M. a desk clerk at the Colorado Springs Holiday Inn, located only across the street from the abandoned van and the Quality Inn that the cops had searched earlier that day, called the Colorado Springs police. The clerk said that a man in a hooded jacket checked in that evening and paid cash for a room, and offered to pay extra for a room on the ground floor. The clerk told the police that the man was staying in Room 426.

The police, as quietly as possible, converged on the Holiday Inn at approximately nine P.M. Officer Tom Stevens of the Colorado Springs Police Department walked quietly down the hallway with five SWAT members following closely behind him. Stevens, with his gun drawn, nervously knocked on the door to Room 426. There was no response. He made three more futile attempts to get someone to answer the door, but it was no use. If Murphy and Newbury were in that room, they weren't going to answer the door. Stevens and the SWAT team retreated down the hall and waited.

Meanwhile, Detective James Stinson placed a telephone call to the room, but again there was no answer. As they waited quietly and were discussing their next plan of action, a front desk clerk called the investigators. A man in Room 426, the clerk said, had just called the front desk to inquire whether or not someone from the hotel had been trying to call his room. One of the detectives immediately called the room again, and this time a man answered.

"My name is Patrick Murphy," the man told the detective. "I've been in Texas prisons for a long time. I don't know how you did this, but you got us." Murphy indicated that he had some demands, and asked to speak to a supervisor. While he was speaking, the officer heard the familiar sound of a pump action shotgun in the background being readied for firing.

The police quickly evacuated the wing of the hotel where Murphy and Newbury were holed up, and SWAT sharpshooters converged on the hotel. As an added measure they cut off the electricity to that part of the hotel, and waited for negotiators to arrive.

It was ten P.M. when the negotiators arrived. The team consisted of FBI negotiators as well as Matt Harrell, Tom Harris, Tina Wisler, and Alan Baccarella of the Colorado Springs police. After learning that Newbury was in the room with Murphy, Harrell talked with Murphy over the next five hours about their demands.

Their demands turned out to be a singular request, and it was a relatively simple one—Murphy and Newbury wanted to speak to MSNBC News, a cable network, and make a statement on national television before giving themselves up. Unfortunately, none of the police officers knew anyone at MSNBC, but they went to work to try and satisfy the demand with an alternative. They finally settled on a five-minute interview via telephone for each of the fugitives on live television with local KKTV news anchorman Eric Singer. After the details of the deal were worked out, Murphy and Newbury went on the air with Singer at 3:35 A.M. and voiced their displeasure with the manner in which the State of Texas runs it penal system. Their statements basically consisted of an indictment of the Texas prison system, which they accused of being "just as corrupt as we are."

When each man had their five minutes with the news anchorman, they removed their shirts, as instructed, and surrendered peacefully to the police waiting for them outside their room. They were escorted out of the hotel and placed in waiting patrol cars.

Back in Texas, relief seemed to be the word of choice after the capture of the remaining fugitives. In Kenedy, many of the residents claimed that they would sleep better knowing that the convicts were back behind bars. But they also expressed feelings of unease about living so close to the Connally Unit after what had occurred. It could happen again, many people said.

"We're very excited," said one elderly female resident. "I can sleep in peace now."

"We're just glad they didn't kill anybody else," said another elderly female resident after hearing news of the capture.

"It's the greatest thing that ever happened," said an elderly man. "Women who live down here wouldn't even go inside their houses until the law came and opened their doors to make sure it was okay."

In Irving, citizens expressed similar feelings.

"I am just very thankful and our prayers are beginning to be answered," said Irving Chamber of Commerce President James Spriggs. "We just had so much concern in our city over what they did to Officer Hawkins."

"It's hard to put into words when an officer is killed in the line of duty during the holidays," said Hawkins's training officer, Jose Rios. "It's a lot to deal with. It's just hard . . . we all take it personal. It doesn't bring it to an end yet, but it's starting to bring it to an end."

"My immediate reaction is sadness because it makes it real," said Jayne Hawkins, who said that she had not been able to think of much besides the prison escapees who killed her son. "And [before] they were

. . . caught, it still wasn't really real for some reason."

Mrs. Hawkins said that she has been channeling her blame toward prison officials instead of the escapees. "You expect criminal behavior from criminals," she said. "I hope they can keep them in jail, and I swear I'm not being facetious.

Because she feels that the escapees can not feel the pain that she has felt over the loss of her son, she does not wish to speak to them. She does, however, want to see them.

"Do I want to see them?" she asked. "Only because I want them to see me. Of course they are psychopaths so they have no conscience whatsoever, but they are going to see me. They will look at me, and I want to see what they look like when they look at the mother of a child who is gone."

CHAPTER
18

Although the police were satisfied that they had done their job by getting the remaining six of the Texas 7 fugitives back behind bars where they belonged, they also knew that their work was not over yet. They still had to resolve the issue of whether the escapees had outside help. Everyone associated with the case believed that they did receive some kind of assistance, but what and by whom?

"Somebody called and warned them that we might be out for them," said Commander James Rocco of the Woodland Park Police Department. "That makes you pucker when you hear that." Rocco, as well as many of the others, couldn't get the cellular phone call they intercepted out of their minds.

The phone call in question, said Rocco, had been the first indication that the group might have received outside assistance while in Colorado. After Newbury and Murphy had been taken into custody, the police went back to Randy Halprin and questioned him about it and he readily admitted that he had received that call.

"He told the agents he received a phone call from the roadblock," Rocco said. Although Rocco did not reveal whether Halprin had told the investigators who had called him, he did say that he did not believe that the call came from either Murphy or Newbury. The FBI believed, said Rocco, that since Murphy and Newbury had left the group over the weekend, it didn't seem likely that they could be aware of the capture of Rivas, Rodriguez, and Garcia, or of the planned siege on the RV park.

Bolstering his belief that the fugitives had help from others, Rocco learned that they had visitors during the time they stayed at the park. Because the visitors' identities were not known, there was no way for anyone to easily determine whether they were recent acquaintances or old friends from the past.

"There's somebody on the outside," Rocco said with certainty. "I don't know if it's a local or not."

Rocco learned that a number of the park's residents had told police, after the fugitives' arrests, that they sometimes had visitors during the evening hours. However, none of the residents recognized any of the visitors.

One of the reasons that the escapees were able to elude capture for so long, Rocco and other investigators reasoned, was their apparent ingenuity in realizing that they would draw less attention to themselves if they went out regularly and tried to blend into the community. People would likely have become suspicious of them if they had remained quiet, behind locked doors all of the time.

One example of their attempts at trying to blend in occurred soon after their arrival in the Pueblo area. Donald Newbury decided he wanted a new change of clothes, so he stopped into a Western Wearhouse and began looking at coveralls. He couldn't find his size, so he struck up a conversation with a salesman who helped him find what he was looking for.

"By the way, what do you do for a living?" the salesman had asked, to make small talk.

"I used to work in a prison," Newbury responded. "I didn't like what I was doing, so I decided to go into construction." Newbury paid cash for the coveralls and left, and the salesman hadn't raised an eyebrow at the time over what Newbury had said. He had seemed like such a normal, ordinary guy to the salesman, and it wasn't until after the arrests had been made, and he'd seen his customer on the news, that the salesman recalled his conversation with Newbury. The salesman had been shocked, like just about everyone else, when he saw that the FBI had removed ten handguns, including the one that had belonged to Officer Aubrey Hawkins, two shotguns, and lots of ammunition from the Holiday Inn room where Newbury was staying when he and Murphy surrendered.

As the investigators continued to piece together details of the fugitives' journey, they learned of an event that seemed very much out of character for such hardened criminals as the Texas 7. While still in Pueblo, Larry Harper, the religious one, attended a service at the Word of Jesus Christ Church. During the service the pastor requested prayers for two church members who were having severe financial difficulties and were in need of a car.

A few days later the pastor's wife discovered a car title and a set of car keys inside the church's mailbox. There was a note attached which read: "May God bless you as He has blessed us." The note also included written instructions to a Motel 6 in Pueblo where the car, a 1986 Honda, was located. When she arrived, she found that the keys fit, and it started right up. As she was driving away she noticed the curtains move in one of the motel's upper level rooms and she felt that someone was watching her. Nervous and a little suspicious over the entire ordeal, she called the police to find out if the car had been stolen. To her surprise, she learned that the car had been purchased legally from an individual in a small town in Texas. It had never occurred to her at the time that the gift might have come from the Texas 7. However, she learned later, after the arrests had been made, that the Texas 7 had driven the car from Texas to Colorado after buying it. According to the police, they had also stayed at the Motel 6 in Pueblo before moving on to Woodland Park.

Piecing together the trail of the Texas 7 was not an easy task, and it was made all the more difficult because of the apparent incongruity, at least on the surface, of witnesses' statements that placed them at particular locations on given dates. Wade Holder had told the police that the fugitives checked into his RV park on January 1, yet investigators had placed them in Pueblo as early as late December and as late as January 11. The clothing salesman had guessed that it had been in late December or early January that Donald Newbury had come into his store, and the pastor and his wife said that Larry Harper had come to a service at their church on January 7. It had been four days later, on January 11, that the pastor's wife had found the keys to the Honda in the church's mailbox, and in their backtracking, the investigators had been able to place them at the Pueblo Motel 6, where they had registered under assumed names, until December 31.

However, Pueblo was only about an hour down the freeway from Woodland Park, making it possible, even likely, that they had traveled back and forth between the two locations for a while. It also seemed plausible that they had used that setup to meet with the person or persons who the police believed were providing them with outside help.

Delineating their time in Texas following the breakout from the Connally Unit proved to be more difficult. While it was possible to place them at specific locations on certain dates—the Radio Shack in Pearland on December 15 and the Oshman's Sporting Goods store on December 24, for instance—the gaps would be next to impossible to fill in, unless the convicts decided to talk.

Murphy and Newbury, of course, had already started talking. It was through their televised statement, in part, that investigators were able to learn when the seven actually left Texas. Newbury had described driving through a blizzard for hours that began in the Amarillo area on Christmas Eve. However, when the investigators checked the National Weather Service's records for the Amarillo area on Christmas Eve and Christmas day, they learned that only trace amounts of snow had fallen in that area. The so-called "blizzard" had not hit until December 26, during which there were snow accumulations of nearly 17 inches. So where had they really been on December 24 and 25 after fleeing Oshman's?

During the gap between December 15 and December 24, the police had good reason to believe they were in Houston on at least one of those ten days, that of December 18, a Monday. It was on that evening at about 9:30 that three men, each armed with a handgun, held up an Auto Zone store in Pasadena, a Houston suburb, after binding three employees with duct tape. They stole cash and a car. Although the police had not connected the robbery to the Texas 7 officially, it was similar to other heists committed by Rivas.

"One of the suspects put on an Auto Zone shirt and stood at the front door," said Pasadena police sergeant Mike Baird. "It was close to closing time, and it was similar to things that Rivas and his outlaw gang did before he went to prison."

Baird pointed out that Rivas had been known to rob prior places of employment, and he had once worked at an Auto Zone in El Paso.

Similarities in Rivas's modus operandi included: wearing of employees' shirts, stealing an employee's vehicle, and communicating with an accomplice via walkie-talkie. All had been done during the Auto Zone robbery. Although the Auto Zone employees had been unable to identify the escapees when shown a photo, a sketch artist's composite drawings based on the employees' descriptions bore a resemblance to three of the fugitives. However, the Texas 7 have not officially been linked to that robbery.

As the timeline of their journey moved forward, according to the FBI, the fugitives arrived in Pueblo, Colorado on December 26, after what would be a six-hour drive in normal weather conditions. They were driving in two vehicles—a white Chevrolet Suburban and a Honda sedan. After leaving Pueblo, the fugitives arrived in Colorado Springs on December 31, where they purchased a used Pace Arrow motor home for an undetermined amount of money. They then drove west for less than an hour into the mountainous region, where they checked into the Coachlight RV Park in Woodland Park. Somewhere along the way they picked up a silver Jeep Cherokee.

On January 5, Rivas and two of the other fugitives returned to Colorado Springs, where they met up with the owner of a tile-laying business who had a brown 1982 Ford Econoline van for sale. He wanted $1,500 for the van, but Rivas talked him down to $1,320, at which time the seller agreed to sign over the title. The seller thought it was strange that Rivas did not sign the title as well, and when he asked him about it Rivas said he would fill in the name of a church later on.

As the investigators examined the time the fugitives spent inside their RV at the trailer park, they learned that they had ordered out for pizza regularly from a nearby shop called Fast Eddy's and had consumed a lot of beer as they watched movies such as *The Terminator* and *Saving Private Ryan*. As time went on, the investigators believed that their traveling Christian façade began to fade and, toward the end, just before their capture, they had decided to split up into two groups. Each group, according to the FBI, apparently had plans of its own.

Rivas, Garcia, Halprin, Harper, and Rodriguez, the investigators believed, were making plans to go to Denver where they could purchase phony identification and obtain jobs. Murphy and Newbury, on the other hand, had packed up their small arsenal of weapons and ammunition and were on their way to Denver to purchase body armor. The purpose for which it would be used, of course, was anybody's guess. But given their reputations, the arsenal, and the fact that they had all been involved in a murder made their plans, whatever they were, seem all the more sinister. One thing seemed a certainty—that Newbury and Murphy had taken the brown van and had split off permanently from the other five.

CHAPTER

19

Although George Rivas initially denied that the Texas 7 had any outside help in the prison break, or in their journey to Colorado afterward, the investigation was indicating otherwise. Authorities in Texas believed at least one of the inmates had made a telephone call after they escaped. And they may have arranged, days or weeks before the escape, to have someone on the outside have a getaway car waiting for them. The getaway car, investigators believed, was a 1989 Suburban that had been delivered to the Wal-Mart parking lot in Kenedy, Texas. It was subsequently recovered from a car dealership in Colorado Springs after the arrests were made.

Similarly, Colorado investigators began probing

the possible involvement of two people, a woman who worked at a massage parlor frequented by Newbury and Murphy, and a convicted drug dealer, both of whom the police suspected of helping Newbury and Murphy after they broke away from the rest of the group. Police believed the convicted drug dealer assisted Murphy and Newbury in renting the room at the Holiday Inn, but he denied any involvement in the case.

In the meantime, and only days after his arrest, George Rivas began talking, so much talking that a Texas judge would eventually issue a gag order to keep him, his attorneys, and prosecutors, from revealing anything else to the public about his case. He had been charged with robbery, kidnapping, capital murder for killing a cop, and a host of other charges related to his escape from prison and the robberies committed afterward. It was in his best interest to keep quiet, and the judge who issued the gag order wanted to make certain that he received a fair trial. However, before the gag order was issued, he talked to reporters from *The Denver Post*, the Associated Press, *The Fort Worth Star-Telegram,* as well as a number of others, and made a jailhouse appearance on CBS's *60 Minutes* in an interview with Ed Bradley.

"There's a saying in the prison," Rivas told Bradley as he explained how he could no longer bear to be locked up. "It goes: 'I'm sick and tired of being sick and tired.' I got to that point. You know, I didn't want to die an old man in prison is what it comes down to. But take away hope from men, you give 'em an initiative and they are practically unstoppable."

Among the things that Rivas revealed was that the group had remained united until shortly before the end, when Newbury and Murphy wanted to break off and go their own way.

"We had disagreements and conflicts of interest," Rivas said, "but we always resolved them as best as we could. We already had been through so much together. We could have stayed that way for a while. We just wanted to get jobs and try to be normal."

He said that even though Murphy and Newbury had decided to go their own way, the remaining five had maintained their unity.

Rivas also admitted killing Aubrey Hawkins, and took responsibility for his death. He said that at the time of the shooting, Murphy was across the street from the sporting goods store waiting in their Suburban to make the getaway, and that Halprin was walking out of the store with a bag full of clothes.

Rivas described how he was loading the weapons stolen from Oshman's into the back of the manager's Ford Explorer when he suddenly experienced a "gut feeling" that something bad was going to happen. It was Murphy who had seen Hawkins arrive from his vantage point in the Suburban, and he had radioed the others that a police car was coming around the building.

When Rivas saw Hawkins approaching in his patrol

car, he said that he used the walkie-talkie to summon the others from the store. He said he pulled a gun they had stolen from the prison and fired two warning shots first when Hawkins pulled up at the back of the store, and a third shot that hit Hawkins's bulletproof vest when he thought he saw Hawkins reaching for his gun. He said that he saw the bullet mushroom into the officer's Kevlar vest.

"I know I fired into the vehicle three times," Rivas said. "Whether I fired the lethal round that did kill Mr. Hawkins or not, I did initiate it. I am at fault and I do take full responsibility for it.

"I was screaming at him to raise his hands," he stated. "I pray every day that I could get his face out of my mind. It shouldn't have happened, it wasn't supposed to happen . . . I've never done something like that before . . . in all honesty, it is my fault . . ."

He described how Hawkins had begun to cooperate and had raised his hands, his palms facing outward, and how he, Rivas, began walking toward him to handcuff him. It was at about that time that additional gunfire erupted, and Rivas was hit by a bullet on the left side of his abdomen. Although he said that he did not know who had fired those shots, it was right afterward that he fired three more shots, each of which hit Hawkins. He said that he didn't know why he shot Hawkins again, but said that it was not out of anger. He did not offer an explanation why Hawkins was run over three times as they made their getaway. Rivas said that he was shot again, in the thigh, as he climbed into the getaway car. He said that after getting away from the scene of the crime, he closed his own wounds by sewing them up with dental floss.

Rivas said that he didn't plan to fight extradition to Texas, and that if he is convicted of Hawkins's murder and receives the death penalty he hopes it brings some kind of comfort or relief to his mother, Jayne Hawkins.

"I hope it gives comfort or peace to her to know that I'm not going to fight this," Rivas said, adding that he fully expects to receive the death penalty. ". . . No amount of apologies could make up for what I have done. Except that I hope that by me now confessing to this and admitting to my guilt I can give them some sort of closure when my life is taken . . ."

Rivas explained that he chose the other six inmates to escape with him because they, like him, wanted to start over with new lives and new identities.

"There's security in numbers," he said. "And we knew each other. Whatever weaknesses one of us had, the more people that stuck together, the more strength we had . . . I had no hope of parole or ever having a chance to be with my family or with my sons. After hearing what these other men spoke about individually, I basically created a plan . . ."

Rivas said that he chose the other six men based on their character, and wanted people that he knew he could trust. He claimed that the planning for the breakout only took about three weeks, a stark contrast to what prison officials had claimed.

After initially denying that they had outside help, Rivas told a news reporter that they had help getting the Suburban. Claiming that he did not want to implicate his friend, he admitted that one of the other six inmates had arranged for the Suburban to be waiting at the Wal-Mart when they arrived.

Rivas explained that they had not gone to Mexico like the authorities had expected them to do because they felt like they would not have fit in there and that they would have felt lost. When asked if he had any regrets, he said that he had many.

"My best friend is dead," said Rivas, "and Mr. Hawkins is dead, and my friends are now back in prison."

Randy Halprin also spoke to the media, claiming that he and Murphy didn't fire their guns during the Oshman's robbery, and that he and Murphy hadn't even drawn their weapons. He said that the others were firing their guns as they exited the building, and that he had actually started to run away from the scene when one of the escapees called to him. When he turned around, he said one of them accidentally shot him in the foot.

"My heart really goes out to the [Hawkins] family," Halprin said. "I just want them to know that I really wish it didn't happen this way."

Halprin also denied that he had written one of the letters that was left in the prison's guardhouse that read, "You haven't heard the last of us yet," despite having been identified as the writer.

"I never made any threatening statements," Halprin said. "I wish they would produce this letter that said I wrote that statement, because I never did."

Halprin also told reporters that he was not the inmate who had bluffed his way into the guard tower at the prison's back gate, and insisted that Rivas was the inmate who had done that. He stated that his part in the prison break was that of a lookout. He also countered what Rivas had said about the planning of the prison break only taking three weeks. He said that it was six months in the making, more in line with what the prison officials had estimated, and said that Rivas had approached him about the idea as early as April or May of 2000.

Halprin said that Rivas chose Murphy and Newbury to be a part of the plan because it was common knowledge that the guards trusted them. When asked who had supplied the Suburban for the getaway, Halprin said that he did not know. He said that Rivas had asked the group not to ask any questions about it because he did not want to cause any trouble for the person's "family member."

Halprin indicated that the prison break had originally been planned to occur on December 12, but it was postponed because the prison truck they needed had not arrived as scheduled. When the truck showed up the next day, the plan went forward. He said that despite the fact that they had made shanks, the escape plan did not include any acts of violence.

In the meantime, Halprin and four of the remaining

six fugitives indicated through their attorneys that they would fight extradition to Texas. Rivas was the only member of the group who would not. Plans were being initiated to begin extradition proceedings, which could take anywhere from 30 to 60 days to complete. Rivas, however, was returned to Texas within ten days, arriving in the first week of February.

According to Dallas County District Attorney Bill Hill, the state would seek the death penalty for each of the inmates, and he planned to be involved personally in their prosecutions. Hill indicated that he might seek a separate trial for each inmate.

"When you have an escaped convict that's in prison for all types of violations of the law and gets out and kills a police officer, there can't be any more serious type of a crime that would warrant the death penalty, in our opinion," Hill said. "I made the promise to the Dallas Police Department when I spoke to them that if, God forbid, a police officer is ever killed I would be involved in the case . . . we started looking at this case the day after it happened, in terms of the evidence and the defendants. In the back of our minds, we always knew that was what we were going to do."

CHAPTER
20

While the extradition proceedings were underway for the five remaining fugitives being held without bail in Colorado, Rodriguez and Garcia were having second thoughts about fighting extradition and they indicated through their attorneys that they would make a decision by February 22.

In the meantime Colorado authorities revealed that Michael Rodriguez had admitted shooting officer Hawkins. The revelation was discovered in a letter that he wrote to a woman in Texas while in jail. According to Teller County Sheriff Frank Fehn, Rodriguez had referred to the letter's recipient as his wife.

"In the letter, he made the admission that he shot officer Hawkins in the head and dragged him out of the car," Fehn said. Fehn would not reveal any additional information about the letter's contents, but added that it had been turned over to investigators in Texas.

As the investigation continued into whether the convicts had outside help, little information was being released to the public. John Moriarty, an investigator with the TDCJ and an operations manager for the inspector general's office of that entity, did indicate, however, that one or more arrests were expected. They appeared to be concentrating their efforts on finding out who left the Suburban at the Wal-Mart, whether any cash or fake identification documents were left in the vehicle for the escapees, and whether or not contact was made with anyone to obtain the keys to the vehicle.

Part of Moriarty's job involves investigating the prison breaks themselves, a task that he has been doing for the department since the late 1980s. In this case, he found that what made the Connally Unit break so unusual was the planning done by the inmates and the likely outside assistance.

"Typically, the inmates have a great plan that takes them to the fence, but beyond that they don't have a plan," Moriarty said. "This plan went beyond the fence. It was well thought out." He said that he had not found anything in his investigation that indicated the prisoners had any help from any of the prison's employees.

According to Moriarty, Michael Rodriguez had attempted a previous escape from another prison, the Coffield Unit, before he was transferred to the Connally Unit. Rodriguez's plan had been simple and pale in comparison to the Connally Unit breakout. He'd had no help from the outside, there was no overpowering of the guards or other employees, and there wasn't an escape vehicle involved. He had simply tried to hide in one of the prison's buildings until he could figure out how to get outside the gate. It was Rodriguez, in fact, who had initially contacted Rivas about breaking out of the Connally Unit. However, Rivas rejected his plan because he considered it too desperate and felt it would not work. Afterward, Rivas began planning the escape himself.

Rumors had been circulating that letters had been written in code to a relative or a friend of one of the inmates in the Connally Unit break, but Moriarty would not comment about that aspect of the breakout. He did say that the prison system did not routinely track information regarding whom inmates write to, but the investigation had been able to compile a list of inmate friends and relatives from viewing visitors lists.

Although Newbury and Murphy and been getting a lot of attention in the aftermath of their capture regarding the statements they had made on television, prison officials had no comment regarding the five minutes of news time that had been afforded to them. Normally criminals attempt to manipulate the media for their own ends, particularly with regard to what Halprin was saying. But Murphy and Newbury used their time to criticize the Texas prison system and the judicial system in general.

"The judicial system in the State of Texas has really gone to the pits," Newbury had said. "We're receiving 99 years for a robbery for [a $68 holdup], and nobody's injured. There's no proof a gun was used in the robbery other than an unreliable witness who picked out several IDs and everything before, who created a statement through information in my files . . . that apparently the prosecutor had given him, which is strictly against the law as well . . . they're giving kids so much time that they will never get to see light again. Their life is gone. Now all they are is a roach in a cage. Things have to be changed, there has to be more rehabilitation in the system down there . . ."

Although the news media chose to have a field day with their comments and condemnation of the Texas prison system, little was said of the fact that all of the Texas 7 were hardened criminals and deserved the imprisonment for the crimes that they had committed. Despite the flaws that obviously exist within the Texas prison system and the judicial system in general, it should be remembered that these men are not heroes, or even legends, because of their successful escape from a maximum-security prison. They are murderers, thieves, rapists, and a child abuser.

Shortly after his arrival in Dallas on Thursday, February 1, George Rivas, accompanied by U.S. marshals, was brought to the Dallas jail in a white van with heavily tinted windows amid tight security. A convoy of six Dallas County Sheriff's Department patrol cars escorted the van, while hovering television news helicopters watched. A short time later he was arraigned before a Dallas County magistrate on the charge that he murdered Irving police officer Aubrey Hawkins. Handcuffed and shackled by a chain around his waist, he acknowledged that he understood the charges against him when asked by Magistrate Dorothy Shead. Afterward he signed an affidavit that declared him indigent, which qualified him for a court-appointed attorney. Although his bail was set at $1 million, he would not be allowed to post bail, even if he somehow obtained it, because of his status as an escaped felon. Following the arraignment, he was fingerprinted and photographed, and isolated in a cell inside the Lew Sterrett Justice Center. As a matter of convenience, he would be held in the jail to await his trial instead of being sent back to prison.

It was noted that Rivas, and the remaining members after their eventual return to Texas, would be isolated from the rest of the jail's population as well as each other because of the apparent strength they seemed to garner when communicating with each other.

A short time later State District Judge Molly Francis, the presiding judge in the case, scheduled a preliminary hearing to consider, among other things, whether she would impose a gag order on the case because of her concern over all of the media interviews that had been conducted with the escapees.

"As far as I know, she just wants to have the hearing because she's concerned about everything she's heard on the news," said Kerry Young, a staff attorney for the county who performs legal work for a number of the district judges. "What they're trying to accomplish is to avoid polluting potential jury pools."

CHAPTER
21

Although their motivation was not known, Donald Newbury and Patrick Murphy, Jr. went before El Paso County (Colorado) District Judge Gilbert Martinez and announced that they no longer wanted to fight extradition to Texas. Both inmates told the judge that they freely waived their right to challenge extradition. Plans were immediately implemented to have U.S. marshals return the convicts to Texas by February 26. Joseph Garcia, Michael Rodriguez, and Randy Halprin, however, remained steadfast in their plans to fight extradition.

In another development, Colorado prosecutors announced that they would not be pressing charges against the massage parlor employee and the convicted drug dealer that police had suspected of providing help to Murphy and Newbury. Although the investigation had shown that the convicted drug dealer had rented the Holiday Inn hotel room for the two fugitives, there was not enough proof that showed either of the people had any prior knowledge of who the inmates were. Under Colorado law, proof is required that an alleged accessory actually knew that the person they were assisting had committed a crime or was wanted by authorities for a crime.

"We don't have any charges based on the investigation thus far," David Gilbert, a prosecutor with the El Paso County District Attorney's Office, said. "There is insufficient evidence to prove beyond a reasonable doubt that either were aware of the identity of the two Texas fugitives at the time they were voluntarily assisting them in renting motel rooms."

The investigation in Colorado revealed that the massage parlor employee had fallen in love with Newbury in the days before his surrender, but that she had no prior knowledge of his true identity. In her presence, Murphy and Newbury had referred to themselves as "Ronnie" and "John," and that was how the massage parlor employee had introduced them to the drug dealer. It was only after seeing a television news report while in their room at the Holiday Inn that the massage parlor employee learned their true identities. After seeing the report, Newbury and Murphy told her their names and provided information about their pasts.

It was soon revealed that Randy Halprin had mailed a letter to a Texas newspaper shortly after his arrest, in which he talked about plans of leaving Colorado after obtaining phony identification. He claimed that he had always been inspired by music, and he planned to go to Seattle to begin a new life as a grunge musician.

"That's my passion, music," Halprin wrote in the letter. "I just wanted to start a new life . . . I felt I could blend in there and be able to start my life from the ground up . . . all I was waiting on were the IDs that Donald Newbury and Patrick Murphy were working on in Colorado Springs. They were to come back on Tuesday, give us the IDs, and then I was leaving. I was tired of being a Texas 7."

At another point, Halprin reiterated to news reporters in Colorado that he had not fired any of the shots that killed Aubrey Hawkins during the Oshman's robbery, and expressed his trepidation about facing the death penalty upon his return to Texas.

"It hasn't really sunk in yet," Halprin told a reporter. "I don't want to die. I don't want to be strapped down like an animal . . . I'm not this horrible guy. I just wanted to start a new life."

Meanwhile, as preparations got underway to bring the remaining inmates back to Texas for trial, state government officials were estimating that it would cost taxpayers as much as $3 million, or more, to house

the criminals and bring them to trial. Texas governor
Rick Perry pledged that his office would award Dallas
County a $250,000 grant, taken from the state's dis-
cretionary funds, to be applied toward the trials.

"Dallas County faces extraordinary challenges in
bringing these men to trial," Perry said, "and this
grant will help ensure that justice is carried out.

Others, however, like State Representative Do-
mingo Garcia, said the grant, while "an important first
step," was not enough. Along those lines Garcia has
introduced a bill asking the state legislature to appropriate $1.1 million to go toward the costs of the trials.

"We will be talking to the district attorney and the
county judge to determine whether to proceed with a
larger appropriation from the state general revenue
funds," Garcia said, adding that he was taking such
actions because the men being tried broke out of a
state prison.

"The only connection these convicts have with Dallas County is that they killed a police officer here,"
Garcia said. "These were state prisoners, and the State
of Texas has an obligation to police officers throughout the state to show that we're going to help bring
these people to justice and we're going to help pay
for it when one of our people escapes."

As all of the legal wrangling surrounding the Texas
7 continued almost nonstop, investigators in Texas
continued focusing their attention on the San Antonio
area in their attempts to identify the person or persons

they believed helped the inmates after their escape.

"We are focusing our investigation down there in San Antonio," said TDCJ investigator John Moriarty. That attention, he said, was being aimed at the 1989 Suburban. "We have learned that the vehicle was sold in San Antonio a couple of days before the escape."

Specifically, they were trying to learn who drove the Suburban from San Antonio to the Wal-Mart parking lot in Kenedy, and how the driver was able to return to San Antonio. Moriarty said that his investigators believed that the inmates drove the vehicle to San Antonio and stayed overnight in a motel there before moving on to the Houston area. After committing the robbery at the Pearland Radio Shack, and possibly robbing the Auto Zone store in Pasadena, investigators believe that they drove the Suburban to the Dallas area where they committed the Oshman's robbery and murder in nearby Irving before driving on to Colorado where they sold the vehicle to a used car dealer in Colorado Springs.

"The vehicle was impounded and processed by the FBI's evidence response team out of Colorado Springs," Moriarty said. As they continued to backtrack and follow the leads associated with the Suburban, investigators learned that an individual in San Antonio had sold it to a Hispanic man and woman believed to be in their forties or fifties.

"We believe it was left in the Wal-Mart parking lot within 48 hours of the escape," Moriarty said. The focus now, he said, was on learning the identities of the couple that purchased the vehicle.

In the aftermath of the Connally Unit breakout, and the subsequent capture of the remaining fugitives, many people, including prison officials, began to question whether the hard line taken against offenders in Texas has contributed to recent prisoner unrest. There was indeed a new breed of inmates who were younger, tougher, and more violent than prisoners in years past. And they were now serving longer sentences. They had less reason to consent to prison rules and a greater incentive to try escaping. This was certainly not intended when voters and the Legislature decided to get tough on offenders. Such prisoners, who have little hope of parole before middle age, are creating a higher management risk for prison officials and correctional officers.

"If a 20-year-old gets a 50-year sentence for an aggravated crime, we know we're going to have him for 25 years," said Gary Johnson, TDCJ's director of the Institutional Division. "They can't even fathom 25 years because they haven't been alive that long. With someone who is 18 or 19, in all likelihood their parole officer has not yet been born . . . the risk of them wanting to get out is going to be greater."

Johnson's statement was echoed in the statements that Donald Newbury and Patrick Murphy, Jr. provided shortly before they surrendered. Today, it was pointed out, a violent offender in the state of Texas typically would serve more than 70 percent of his or her sentence before he or she would be eligible for parole. In 1990, that figure had been 30 percent. In 1999, less than one out of four inmates eligible for parole were actually paroled, compared to 10 years earlier when nearly four out of every five eligible for parole were approved. Not only has time off for good behavior been virtually eliminated under the current rules, but the waiting periods between parole hearings are longer.

There are other problems associated with the get-tough stance. During the past decade, prison populations have increased at least three times over, and the corresponding rate of assaults against prison staff and corrections officers has increased ten times.

"[The inmates] get to the point [where] they get into so much trouble on the unit, they've got nothing to lose by attacking an officer, creating havoc and causing as many problems on the unit as they can because they know they're going to be there for a long, long time and the good time's been taken away," said Brian Olsen, director of the union that represents correctional officers, in a reference to the younger, more violent prisoners.

"An inmate who comes into the institutional division can gain privileges or lose privileges based on his or her behavior," Johnson said, referring to the behavior management tools they have left to work with. "That would be everything from contact visitation, phone calls to family, the number of visits every month, the amount of money you can spend in the commissary, how much recreation you get, the type of job you can get—we still have all that."

In an effort to deter attacks and to make their jobs safer, Texas officials now allow officers who work alone to carry containers of protective chemical agents, such as Mace and pepper spray. The prison system has also begun providing stab-proof vests for the officers, and is now purchasing body alarms as well.

To every question and problem, Texas prison officials seem to be ready with answers—but are they the right answers?

"I argue consistently that it's fine to be tough on crime, and we are the toughest probably in the nation," said state Senator John Whitmire. "But we're not smart on crime . . . most criminals eventually get out."

Others, including criminal justice experts, believe that Texas's approach to punishment is shortsighted. Increasing evidence that shows that prisoners making parole are coming out of the system with a greater criminal mindset than they had when they went in. Some experts believe that Texas needs to offer more rehabilitation programs to its prisoners, especially in the areas of drug abuse and mental illness.

As for the Connally Unit breakout itself, some politicians, such as Lt. Governor Bill Ratliff, believe that lessons can be learned from mistakes.

"I think it is unrealistic for us to believe that we

could ever build a prison system that nobody could escape from, but we could try," Ratliff said. "Sometimes it takes very unfortunate incidents in order to teach us what we need to do differently. Obviously, we need to institute some changes in either the procedures, or rules, or physical facilities, and maybe all of the above, in order to see if we can keep this from happening again."

What was next for the Connally Unit escapees?

According to Mac Stringfellow, chairman of the TDCJ, the inmates would eventually all be returned to Texas, where they would would stand trial for the murder of officer Hawkins. If convicted of capital murder, they could end up on death row.

"They will certainly go into administrative segregation for however long it takes to adjust their attitudes," Stringfellow said.

CHAPTER
22

By Friday, February 2, the mystery surrounding who had supplied the Suburban to the escapees was over. After talking with a couple in San Antonio that the Suburban had been traced back to, investigators learned that it had been sold to a woman named Patsy Gomez, 41, on December 11, two days before the Connally Unit breakout.

They also had another break. A man, whom investigators preferred not to name, came forward and told them that he had accompanied Patsy Gomez when she bought the vehicle. He said that he also accompanied her to the Wal-Mart parking lot where she dropped it off. At that time the man said that he had no idea that the vehicle was connected to the prison escapees, but a few days later, amid all of the publicity, he said that Gomez had told him that the Suburban had been used as the getaway car.

Soon after her name had surfaced, investigators searched a number of sources of public records for a Patsy Gomez. As it turned out, they found a record that showed that she had purchased another vehicle ten years earlier with another man—Raul Rodriguez—who had cosigned the car loan with her. They had finally found the link that they had been looking for to connect one of the relatives of the Texas 7 to aiding the inmates in the breakout. Rodriguez had, after all, visited his son, Michael, at the prison in the days preceding the breakout. It was all beginning to make some sense now.

Investigators quickly secured an arrest warrant for Gomez from a judge in Karnes County, and then located her in a bar in San Antonio. Faced with the evidence and the potential charges against her, she agreed to talk to the investigators. Gomez, who lived in a rented house with two girls and earned money selling flowers at bars and restaurants, soon acknowledged her involvement in supplying the Suburban.

When confronted with the fact that her name had been linked to Raul Rodriguez, Gomez agreed to cooperate. She also implicated Rodriguez, her former employer and a longtime family friend.

"She was up-front," John Moriarty said. "She said she was getting ready to be truthful. She wanted the burden lifted."

The investigators subsequently learned that, after allegedly conspiring with his son in prison, Raul Rodriguez had asked Gomez to help him. Investigators believe that he gave Gomez $3,700 in cash to buy the Suburban that he had found for sale through a classified ad. According to the investigators, Gomez purchased the vehicle and drove it to the Wal-Mart parking lot, accompanied by a male friend—the man who authorities won't identify—who followed her in another vehicle. Once there, investigators said, Gomez placed the Suburban's title and $300 cash beneath a rug in the vehicle, and left its keys in the tailpipe.

The investigators arrested Gomez and took her to jail, charging her with seven felony counts of permitting or facilitating the escape. Afterward, they arrested Rodriguez at his home under identical charges. Both were taken to the Karnes County Jail.

According to an affidavit for the arrest warrants, "(Raul) Rodriguez informed Patsy (Gomez) that he needed the Suburban parked at the Kenedy Wal-Mart by ten A.M. . . . so that his son, Michael, could escape from prison." The affidavit also stated that Gomez placed a red ribbon on the dashboard to mark it for the escapees.

"This case is very, very solid," said TDCJ spokesman Glen Castlebury following the arrests. "It's airtight."

"We knew it had to be someone close, a girlfriend or someone else willing to take that kind of risk," chimed in prison board chairman Mac Stringfellow.

"As far as Mrs. Gomez, I don't know what her motivation was." Stringfellow said that investigators had not uncovered any evidence indicating that Raul Rodriguez had paid her for her services. "I believe today we brought closure, and it is finally over . . . two knew what they were doing and why they were doing it, and two [the person who sold the Suburban to Gomez and Gomez's friend who followed her to deliver it] knew what they were doing, but did not know why they were doing it."

At their arraignment, both handcuffed and shackled with chains, Gomez and Rodriguez were informed of the charges facing them and held on $700,000 bail each, $100,000 for each of the seven counts. If convicted, each faced a possible 20-year prison sentence.

AFTERWORD

In the aftermath of the Texas 7 arrests, suicide, and surrender, it didn't take long for Woodland Park businesses to realize that they could cash in on the notoriety of the fugitives who, by design or as they contended, by random process, had chosen their town as a hiding place.

Within days of the fugitives' arrests, the owner of Tres Hombres Bar and Restaurant, announced that he would be auctioning the pool table used by the fugitives, as well as a table where they ate their meals and drank their Shiner beer.

"You couldn't buy this type of advertising," said the establishment's owner, Darby Howard. Howard said, however, that he would not pay to advertise his restaurant as the place where the fugitives liked to eat and drink. To do that, he said, would glorify them, and he doesn't wish to do that. "People did that with Jesse James, but that was 100 years later."

Another eatery, Fast Eddy's Pizza, claimed that they delivered pizza on a number of occasions to the fugitives' RV. The Texas 7 seemed to prefer large pies with pepperoni, sausage, beef, onions, green peppers, and mozzarella cheese. The establishment's owner later added another helping of cheese to bring the total toppings to seven. He named the new item the "Texas Seven Pizza"; each order came with a mug shot of one of the fugitives on the delivery box. It has since become the shop's best-selling pizza. The cost: $7.99. They also sell T-shirts that commemorate the capture of the Texas 7.

Though the case of the Texas 7 has begun to wind down, it is far from over. The trials for the captured fugitives await them down the road, as do the trials for Raul Rodriguez—who, if convicted, may join his sons in prison—and Patsy Gomez. However, under the protections of the U.S. Constitution, George Rivas, Larry Halprin, Donald Newbury, Patrick Murphy, Jr., Michael Rodriguez, and Joseph Garcia, regardless of the past crimes for which they have been convicted, must be presumed innocent of the charges now facing them until they are convicted in a court of law. The same Constitutional protections, of course, apply to Patsy Gomez and Raul Rodriguez.

For Jayne Hawkins, the case will never be over because of the loss of her son. She and Officer Aubrey Hawkins's family planned to file a wrongful death lawsuit against the State of Texas, and have consulted with prominent Houston attorney Dick DeGuerin.

According to DeGuerin, the aim of the lawsuit is not to seek a large amount of money but rather to emphasize the responsibility of the prison officials at the time of the escape and subsequent killing of Officer Hawkins, and to bring about much-needed change in the prison system.

"Ms. Hawkins is very interested in having the public see just what happened so the necessary changes will be made and [such escapes] will not happen again," DeGuerin said. "She is not as interested in money, although she does want to make sure that Aubrey Hawkins's son, Andrew, has some security for the future."

Jayne Hawkins indicated that it was her goal to make positive changes to a state criminal justice board that has not held up its mission promise to "protect the citizens of Texas." She said that in trying to bring about positive changes she hoped to be able to make some sense over the loss of her son.

"He was fighting for justice for the people of Texas that day," Hawkins said. "The goal is to get changes made in all parts of the criminal justice system. We don't want this to happen again . . . my son will not die in vain."

In the meantime the Texas Legislature was being

urged to address additional pay raises for prison guards to help fill the chronic shortage, and attention was drawn to the current low pay, which is not sufficient to attract, and keep, quality corrections officers.

There was also talk of reviewing and revising policies that currently permit violent offenders with lengthy prison records to get work assignments with minimal supervision.

Finally, the legislature was asked to consider alternative sentencing solutions for nonviolent criminals and those parolees who violate the conditions of their parole, to not only provide relief to a prison system that is at near-capacity but to make it easier to allow violent inmates, such as the Texas 7, to be held more securely. Until such changes are implemented, it is only a matter of time until the next Texas 7–type breakout occurs again.

APPENDIX A

Time Line of Events in the December 13, 2000 Connally Unit Prison Break

The following was included in a "Serious Incident Review" conducted by the Texas Department of Criminal Justice, Institutional Division, after the December 13, 2000 breakout of the Connally Unit maximum-security prison in Kenedy, Texas.

11:20 Maintenance employees returned their offenders to their housing assignments and went to lunch. Mr. P. Moczygemba remained in the Maintenance Department with 6 offenders.

11:30 Mr. P. Moczygemba was subdued by the offenders.

11:45 Mr. Camber and Officer Marroquin returned to the Maintenance Department and were subdued by the offenders.

12:00 Mr. Segura and Mr. Burgess returned to the Maintenance Department and were subdued by the offenders.

12:20 Coach McDowell went to the Maintenance Department, retrieved his tools, and left the area.

12:25 Mr. Garza, Mr. Gilley, and Mr. Haun returned to the Maintenance Department and were subdued by the offenders.

12:40 Mr. Schmidt escorted two [uninvolved] offenders to the Maintenance Department. [All three] were subdued.

12:45 Officer Albert went to the Maintenance Department to get a tool and was subdued by the offenders.

1:00 Mr. L. Moczygemba and an [uninvolved] offender returned to the Maintenance Department. [Both] were subdued.

1:05 Officer Perez [called] the Maintenance Department and [asked] to speak with a supervisor. Officer Perez notified a person who identified himself as "Moczygemba" that it was count time.

1:15 Officer Gips received a call from someone in Maintenance that they were going to install monitors in the picket.

APPENDIX

1:20 Officer Janssen received a call from someone in Maintenance that they were going to install monitors in the backgate gatehouse.

1:35 Fire alarms went off in the Maintenance Department. Officer Perez called the Maintenance Department but received no answer.

1:40 Two males wearing civilian clothing and two males wearing offender clothing approached the backgate. The individuals were allowed into the sally port area and into the gatehouse. Officer Janssen was subdued.

1:45 A male wearing civilian clothing approached the gate exiting the compound and asked to enter the picket to take measurements. Officer Gips was subdued.

1:58 Officer Gips broke loose, returned to the top of the tower and requested assistance over the radio. Officer Gips reported that he saw the white maintenance truck on the perimeter road, going past 19-Building.

2:00 While returning to the unit, Officer Olsen saw the white truck in the downtown area of Kenedy.

4:00 The maintenance truck was found abandoned behind Wal-Mart in Kenedy, Texas.

APPENDIX B

The following are the findings of a "Serious Incident Review" of a fact finding investigation conducted by the Texas Department of Criminal Justice, Institutional Division, after the December 13, 2000 breakout of the Connally Unit maximum-security prison in Kenedy, Texas.

DISCOVERY

SECURITY OPERATIONS AND PROCEDURES

SERIOUS INCIDENT REVIEW—CONNALLY UNIT
DECEMBER 19, 2000

The Connally Unit security procedures were evaluated through a review of all applicable documents, on-site inspections, and interviews with unit security staff.

APPENDIX

Findings

- A review was conducted of all post orders and other policies relating to staffed positions involved in this incident: Backgate Officer Post Order 07.054; Backgate Picket Post Order 07.048; Perimeter Picket Post Order 07.046; Turnout Door Officer Post Order 07.103; Maintenance Officer Post Order 07.053; and Administrative Directive 03.28. The team found that the above post orders were in place, current, and available for staff review at each identified post.

- Post Order 07.048 provides guidelines for backgate picket procedures. The post order states that the backgate picket officer shall ensure all persons entering or exiting the unit through the backgate are properly identified and must present their photo identification card. Additionally, Administrative Directive 03.28 instructs that all uniformed and non-uniformed personnel will be required to show their TDCJ identification card prior to admission to or exit from the facility.

- The backgate picket officer allowed an individual to pass through the exterior gate of the backgate sallyport without properly and positively identifying the person. This is in violation of Post Order 7.048. The backgate picket officer then allowed this unidentified person to enter the picket where weapons are stored and gate controls are secured. The Building Major had been on this picket with this officer, within the previous month of this incident, providing him specific training on proper procedures for the backgate picket.

- A review of the Agency's post orders indicates that there are no specific instructions or procedures that outline identification or authorization requirements prior to allowing individuals into a perimeter picket.

- Offender Rodriguez was able to gain access to Maintenance Department and become an active participant in this incident.

- The maintenance truck had been moved inside the compound on the morning of the incident, at approximately 1037, to be utilized by a staff member for a parts pickup in the afternoon. There was no need for this vehicle to be inside the compound.

- Mr. McDowell went to the Maintenance Department to check-out the 3 Gym toolbox. Offender Rivas told Mr. McDowell that Mr. P. Moczygemba was in 18 Dorm and that there were no other supervisors in the department. Mr. McDowell retrieved his tools, left the area and did not report to security staff that he had encountered offenders that were not under supervision.

- An offender that was not assigned to the tool room issued Mr. McDowell his toolbox. Although the contents of the toolbox did not include sensitive tools (bolt cutters, cutting torches, etc.), Administrative Directive 03.19 states that only offenders assigned to a tool room and authorized personnel shall be permitted access to tools.

- Having taken Mr. P. Moczygemba's keys, the offenders were able to gain access to the Maintenance Department's sensitive tools that are kept in the tool room. Sensitive tools include any tools or equipment likely to be used in an escape attempt or that poses a threat to unit security. See Attachment G for a list of tools that were taken from the tool room.

- The victims set off the fire alarm from within the Maintenance Department at approximately 1335. The Control Picket officer was alerted by the activated alarm and called the Maintenance Department. When there was no answer, she silenced the alarm on her control panel.

- Two officers are normally assigned to the Central Control Picket and were on this date. However, one of the officers had left her post for a period of time and was not in the Central Control Picket when the fire alarm went off. (This remains under review.)

- The pillowcases that were placed over the heads of the victims, were the containers that were used by the laundry department to deliver rags to the departments.

Recommendations

- Although routine practice is for the backgate officer to assist the backgate picket officer in the identification of persons entering and exiting the backgate, Post Orders 07.048 and 07.054 should have specific guidelines requiring these actions at units that have both a backgate picket officer and a backgate officer.

- All current perimeter picket post orders should be revised to include basic requirements of perimeter picket officers to only allow authorized personnel into the picket and only after such personnel has been properly identified by the picket officer. With the exception of the relieving officer upon shift change, anyone needing access to a perimeter picket must be given authorization by a security supervisor.

- The unit administration should review turnout door procedures and ensure only authorized offenders are allowed passage through this area.

- All departments should adhere to the unit administration's instruction and the guidelines outlined in Administrative Directive 03.28, which requires that vehicles remain outside the compound unless vehicle entry is necessary to perform a specific function. In such cases that vehicle should be inside the compound only so long as is necessary to perform that service and only while an employee attends it and then immediately removed from the compound.

- Mr. McDowell should have reported immediately to security staff that the offenders in the Maintenance Department were unsupervised. Unit administration should ensure that all employees are aware of their responsibility to alert security staff upon detection of this type of situation.

- Unit Administration should ensure that all employees are aware of the guidelines outlined in Administrative Directive 03.19. Only employees and offenders that are assigned to a tool room should have access. Additionally, employees should not accept tools from unauthorized personnel or offenders, but should immediately report the violation to a supervisor.

- In accordance with the Connally Unit Fire Plan, the Control Picket officer should have immediately notified a security supervisor.

MAINTENANCE PROCEDURES

Information concerning Operation and Maintenance procedures was obtained through on-site inspections, interviews with staff members and a review of all applicable documents.

Findings

- Through an on-site inspection of the Maintenance Department, it was discovered that the telephone in the Maintenance Supervisor's Office had outside calling capabilities. The office remained locked at all times; however, when the offenders subdued Mr. P. Moczygemba they acquired the key to the office. Although there is no evidence to support this theory, it was the observation of the review team that the assailants could have used this access to make contact with their accomplices to give instruction on the time and place to leave the drop car.

- An offender impersonating a maintenance employee notified the picket officers, that Area Maintenance was coming to install monitors in the sallyport and backgate pickets.

Recommendation

- The Agency should review the feasibility of discontinuing outside calling capabilities to telephones in areas frequented by offenders. If the discontinuation is not feasible, the Agency should review the availability of technology for limiting access to those lines.

- All current perimeter picket post orders should be revised to include basic requirements of perimeter picket officers to only allow authorized personnel into the picket and only after such personnel has been properly identified by the picket officer.

EMERGENCY RESPONSE

Findings

The implementation of the facility's emergency response plan was reviewed and it showed that the escape plan was current, complete, and extremely well coordinated. The unit administration responded immediately and decisively in initiating and implementing the unit's escape plan, deploying appropriate staff, and establishing search areas and perimeters. The coordinated effort by the unit administration with law enforcement entities and support staff from surrounding facilities and within the agency was exceptional.

Recommendation

- None.

STAFFING

The Connally Unit operates under the staffing document of the TDCJ Security Administration and Security Staffing Plan as provided by Security Operations.

APPENDIX

Findings

- The Connally Unit Staffing Plan allocates 526 Correctional Officer positions. Of the 526 positions, 77 were vacant on the day of the incident. Additionally, 16 Correctional Officers were on extended sick leave on the day of the incident.

- The Connally Unit 1st shift is allocated 127 Correctional Officer positions. On the date of the incident, according to card schedules, there were 106 Correctional Officer Positions assigned to 1st shift. Of those 106, 96 were actually on duty at the time of the incident.

- There were 16 maintenance employees assigned to the Maintenance Department on the day of the incident. 3 maintenance employees failed to report for duty due to severe weather conditions, 1 employee did not report for duty due to illness, and 1 employee was assigned to in-service training.

- Prior to the incident, in the morning hours, there were 11 maintenance supervisors and 26 offenders working in the Maintenance Department. This offender to employee ratio was more than sufficient. When the incident began

there was 1 supervisor and 6 offenders working in the Maintenance Department which is
considered adequate.

• The back gate and the backgate picket were
staffed appropriately on the day of the incident.

• Unit staffing was not found to be a contributing factor in this incident.

Recommendation

• None.

CLASSIFICATION

The Serious Incident Review team conducted a thorough review of the classification records of the offenders involved in the incident.

Findings

• Offender Garcia, Joseph C., TDCJ #774391,
was received February 10, 1997, on a 50-year
sentence for Murder with a Deadly Weapon
from Bexar County. He is a 29-year-old Hispanic male. Due to the nature of his offense
and the length of his sentence, he was assigned

to the Connally Unit, a maximum-security facility, on January 27, 1998. Offender Garcia had no history of assaultive or violent behavior while incarcerated in the TDCJ–Institutional Division. At the time of the incident, Offender Garcia was classified as a Minimum-In, State Approved Trustee III offender and was assigned to the Connally Maintenance Department on May 26, 2000 as a Material Handler.

* Offender Rivas, George, TDCJ #702267, was received April 20, 1995, on a life sentence for Aggravated Kidnapping with a Deadly Weapon (8), Aggravated Kidnapping (5), Aggravated Robbery with a Deadly Weapon (1), Aggravated Robbery (2), and Burglary of a Habitation (1) from El Paso County. He is a 30-year-old Hispanic male. Due to the nature of his offense and the length of his sentence, he was assigned to the Connally Unit, a maximum-security facility, on July 13, 1998. Offender Rivas had no history of assaultive or violent behavior while incarcerated in the TDCJ—Institutional Division. At the time of the incident, Offender Rivas was classified as a Minimum-In, State Approved Trustee III offender and was assigned to the Connally Maintenance Department on October 19, 1999 as a Support Service Inmate.

- Offender Rodriguez, Michael Anthony, TDCJ #698074, was received March 16, 1995, on a life sentence for Capital Murder with a Deadly Weapon from Bexar County. He is a 38-year-old Hispanic male. Due to the nature of his offense and the length of his sentence, he was assigned to the Connally Unit, a maximum-security facility, on July 8, 1999. Offender Rodriguez had no history of assaultive or violent behavior while incarcerated in the TDCJ—Institutional Division. However, he was charged with an attempted escape on June 10, 1995 while assigned to the Coffield Unit. He was placed in Administrative Segregation from July 7, 1995 until September 5, 1996 when he was released as a close custody offender to general population on the Coffield Unit. Offender Rodriguez was reclassified to medium custody on December 12, 1996 and to minimum on March 31, 1997. At the time of the incident Offender Rodriguez was classified as a Minimum-In, State Approved Trustee III offender and was assigned to the Connally Unit inside yard squad on April 19, 2000.

- Offender Halprin, Randy Ethan, TDCJ #786259, was received May 30, 1997, on a 30-year sentence for Injury to a Child /Serious

Bodily Injury with a Deadly Weapon from Tarrant County. He is a 23-year-old white male. Due to the nature of his offense and the length of his sentence, he was assigned to the Connally Unit, a maximum-security facility, on June 1, 1999. Offender Halprin had no history of assaultive or violent behavior while incarcerated in the TDCJ—Institutional Division. At the time of the incident, Offender Halprin was classified as a Minimum-In, State Approved Trustee III offender and was assigned to the Connally Unit Maintenance Department on February 9, 2000 as a Material Handler.

• Offender Harper, Larry James, TDCJ #861910, was received March 9, 1999, on a 50-year sentence for Aggravated Sexual Assault (6) and Aggravated Sexual Assault with a Deadly Weapon (3) from El Paso County. He is a 37-year-old white male. Due to the nature of his offense and the length of his sentence, he was assigned to the Connally Unit, a maximum-security facility, on April 8, 1999. Offender Harper had no history of assaultive or violent behavior while incarcerated in the TDCJ—Institutional Division. At the time of the incident, Offender Harper was classified as a Minimum-In, State Approved Trustee III offender and was assigned to the Connally Unit Maintenance Department on April 10, 2000 as a Material Handler.

- Offender Murphy, Patrick Henry Jr., TDCJ #386888, was received November 13, 1984, on a 50-year sentence for Aggravated Sexual Assault with a Deadly Weapon and Burglary of a Building from Dallas County. He is a 39-year-old white male. Due to the nature of his offense and the length of his sentence, he was assigned to the Connally Unit, a maximum-security facility, on July 28, 1995. Offender Murphy had no history of assaultive or violent behavior while incarcerated in the TDCJ—Institutional Division. At the time of the incident, Offender Murphy was classified as a Minimum-In, State Approved Trustee III and was assigned to the Connally Unit Maintenance Department on July 23, 1997 as a Carpenter.

- Offender Newbury, Donald, TDCJ #824631, was received May 15, 1998, on a 99-year sentence for Aggravated Robbery with a Deadly Weapon from Travis County. He is a 38-year-old white male. Due to the nature of his offense and the length of his sentence, he was assigned to the Connally Unit, a maximum-security facility, on July 1, 1998. He had no history of assaultive or violent behavior while incarcerated in the TDCJ—Institutional Division. However, in 1987 Offender Newbury and two fellow offenders attempted to escape from the Travis County Jail. They overpowered two correctional officers and took them hostage. The escape failed. At the time of the incident Offender Newbury was classified as a Minimum-In, State Approved Trustee III offender and was assigned to the Connally Unit Maintenance Department on August 5, 1998 as a Door Closer Mechanic.

• The Connally Unit is a maximum-security unit with a capacity of 2,848, which is an appropriate unit of assignment for the above-named offenders. The offenders were assigned to housing and jobs within the Connally Unit compound. In accordance with the Texas Department of Criminal Justice—Institutional Division Classification Plan, the above-named offenders were appropriately reviewed and classified as Minimum-In offenders. Offenders assigned to minimum-in custody live and work under supervision inside a secure perimeter. All seven of the offenders who escaped lived inside the unit's secure perimeter and were assigned to jobs that required them to work inside the unit's secure perimeter.

Recommendation

• None.

CONCLUSION

Upon review of the circumstances and events that contributed to the escape, it became evident to the review team members that the escape was well planned. Moreover, non-compliance with Agency policy contributed to the successful escape from the compound.

A thorough review of the Classification Plan disclosed that the offenders were properly assigned to the unit, were classified appropriately, and were assigned to appropriate work assignments. It should be noted, that although the offenders were classified as Minimum-in, the Connally Unit is a maximum-security facility.

The unit staffing rosters for the day of the incident were reviewed thoroughly by the team members. It was determined that the escape was not a result of lack of security staff and that all posts in the area were manned that day in accordance with the guidelines established by the Security Staffing Plan.

It appears that approximately two and half hours

lapsed between the time the incident began and the time the incident was reported. The incident began at approximately 1120 when staff and offenders assigned to the Maintenance Department went to lunch. It was normal procedure to close the Maintenance Department for an hour for lunch; believing that maintenance was closed, there would be no reason to check on the department during this time period. At approximately 1230, it would be common practice for the offenders assigned to the Maintenance Department to return to their work assignments; however, an offender impersonated a maintenance employee and made a call to the A Turnout Officer, to notify them that only a skeleton crew should return after lunch. The unit began their count at 1300 and a count was called in from the Maintenance Department, leaving no reason to physically check on the department at this time. During the time period of the escape, there was no need for any staff, other than maintenance employees, to be in the area. Also, due to weather conditions, some routine activities had been cancelled causing even less activity in the area. The escape occurred during the slowest period of the day, during lunch and at count time.

Upon notification of the escape, the unit administration responded in a timely manner and in accordance with the Emergency Response Plan. The assistance of local law enforcement was requested immediately, the appropriate staff was deployed, and search areas and perimeters were established.

APPENDIX

The Unit Administration initiated an investigation immediately after the incident occurred. Pursuant to the findings of the Serious Incident Review and the Unit Incident Review of the escape, the unit Warden will initiate appropriate corrective action to include administrative disciplinary action.